# THE COMING DECLINE OF THE CHINESE EMPIRE

ALSO BY VICTOR LOUIS

*The Complete Guide to the Soviet Union*
(co-author)

# THE COMING DECLINE OF THE CHINESE EMPIRE

VICTOR LOUIS

*with a Dissenting Introduction by*

HARRISON E. SALISBURY

**Times BOOKS**

Published by TIMES BOOKS, a division
of Quadrangle/The New York Times Book Co., Inc.
Three Park Avenue, New York, N.Y. 10016

Published simultaneously in Canada by
Fitzhenry & Whiteside, Ltd., Toronto

Library of Congress Cataloging in Publication Data

Louis, Victor E
The coming decline of the Chinese Empire.

Includes index.
1. Russia—Foreign relations—China. 2. China—
Foreign relations—Russia. I. Title.
DK68.7.C5L67 1979          327.47′051          78-20686
ISBN 0-8129-0819-8

Manufactured in the United States of America

Book design by Margaret M. Wagner
Map by Bernhard H. Wagner

# A DISSENTING
# INTRODUCTION
## by Harrison E. Salisbury

This book commands our attention.

If there ever was a book which should be rated triple-X or perhaps double-Q as a warning to the reader that its contents present a potential peril it is this curious one by an even more curious author, Victor Louis.

The X or Q rating is not a matter of pornography—that is, sexual pornography. There is no sex in Louis' book. What confronts us is political perversity seldom seen. It demands attention not because of what the author says but because of his very special credentials. Although he has denied it, the author has long been known for his KGB connections. It is a book of spurious content, dubious logic, flagrant untruth. But like Hitler's *Mein Kampf* we read it not because we trust the author or believe what he writes but because Victor Louis, as a KGB man, is presenting a rationale intended to justify a Soviet "war of liberation"—God help us—against the People's Republic of China.

Louis is no Hitler but as an operative of one of the most powerful organizations in the Soviet Union his words deserve our special attention. When the KGB sneezes the world sometimes comes down with chills and fever. The Soviet Union may not in fact be planning to "respond" to a call from the "oppressed minorities" of the People's Republic. But the fact that Louis wants us to think she might or wants China to think so is noteworthy.

Victor Louis' comments are particularly relevant in light of China's recent incursion into Vietnam. It would be only natural for Louis to cite this punitive attack on Vietnam as an example of the kind of chauvinistic expansionism which he sees in the contemporary policy of the People's Republic. Certainly antagonism between China and Vietnam has a deep historical root, going back 1,500 years or more, just as Vietnam's quarrels with Cambodia have equally deep and twisted roots. Nationalism is the common denominator of these conflicts just as nationalism lies at the core of the Sino-Soviet conflict which has been inevitably heightened and sharpened by the Indochinese crisis. Certainly the Chinese hope to restore their paramount influence in Indochina at some time in the indeterminate future but that they hope to absorb this area in the manner in which Hitler sought *Lebensraum* in the East would be a total misreading.

First a word about the author. Louis made his public appearance twenty years ago at the height of the Khrushchev liberalization. He and his English wife suddenly entered the small foreign correspondents' circle in Moscow—she a former secretary in the British Embassy and he, of uncertain antecedents, a correspondent improbably writing occasional dispatches for English newspapers.

Louis, it transpired, was Soviet-born and a Soviet citizen. His westernized name derived from a French father who had taken Soviet citizenship. He quickly drew attention by his association with young nonofficial artists who began to make their appearance at that time, acting as a middle man in introducing them and their works to Westerners. Unfortunately, not long after Louis became acquainted with a particular artist, that artist began to have trouble with the political police. Soon knowledgeable foreigners had ample reason to believe that behind Louis' amiability (he was as fawning as a young pup) there lurked something less pleasant.

Nonetheless, he made himself useful to some correspondents. He was able to provide, for a price, documents. For instance, the transcript of a notable session of the Union of Soviet Writers at which the expulsion of Boris Pasternak was voted after he was awarded the Nobel prize for literature for his novel *Doctor Zhivago*. He acquired a pleasant flat in one of the new apartment houses being built in the Cheryomokh section in the outskirts of Moscow; he had a car and drove widely around the Soviet Union; he and his wife put together a guide for foreign motorists; and—unlike other Soviet journalists—he didn't seem to care what he said or with whom he associated. It was the kind of boldness that in the Soviet Union leads only to one conclusion and soon there were those who recalled having been in Stalin's prison camps with Louis, who remembered his having been arrested in the late 40's when working for a foreign embassy as a translator, and who said he had later been a *stukach* (informer) and had run a *kapterka* (store) in a concentration camp.

Louis' career flourished. He and his wife went on trips outside the Soviet Union. He had a country dacha and consumer goods such as few in Russia could match (two swimming pools, two cars, two garden tractors, one large and one small, and a house full of gadgets that would put Hammacher-Schlemmer to shame).

His enterprises widened. When Svetlana Alleyueva, Stalin's daughter, published her *Twenty Letters to a Friend* in the West, Louis acquired a copy of the manuscript she had left behind in her apartment and an album of pictures and peddled them to Western European publishers. It took legal action by Harper & Row to stop Louis' pirated editions. He had a hardly concealed hand in the "smuggling" out of Russia of Nikita Khrushchev's taped memoirs. The reason I put "smuggling" in quotation marks is that Louis was a KGB agent and it is not strictly accurate to say a secret police agent "smuggles" things past his comrades in the border guards.

When Alexander Solzhenitsyn began to run afoul of the Soviet authorities, who should appear unannounced on the rustic doorstep of his country cottage to try to talk to him and to snap some unauthorized photos? Louis then offered in the West a tendentious purported interview with Solzhenitsyn.

Louis had a hand in dozens of less spectacular missions. His travels were not uninteresting. He roamed the world. One month he would be in the United States where, of all places, he was invited to talk at Harvard. The next he would improbably appear in Taiwan and spend an afternoon with Chiang Ching-kuo, son and heir of Generalissimo Chiang Kai-shek. Taiwan was, of course, off limits to Soviet citizens since Nationalist China had no diplomatic relations with Soviet Russia. But there was a certain shock value in permitting Louis to come. It was probably intended to suggest to the People's Republic that the Soviet Union and Taiwan were considering détente. (And that, incidentally, is one of the sly motivations of Louis' present work.)

A bit later Louis turned up in Israel and wrote a series of articles suggesting that after all there was still a chance that Moscow and Tel Aviv could arrive at a mutual understanding. He recalled the fervor with which ɔtalin had welcomed the birth of Israel. All was not lost. The Louis gambit caused some minor waves but little more.

In the autumn of 1969 when Soviet Russia and the People's Republic actually were on the verge of war Louis published several exclusive articles reporting the imminence of hostilities. Was Louis very well informed or was he making waves designed to alarm and disorient the world—and the Chinese?

There is no way to answer these questions but it is against this background that his latest contribution must be evaluated.

The fact to be kept clearly and constantly in mind is that Louis is a long-standing and experienced KGB agent with special functions in the international area, particularly in China. In the last ten years he has, obviously, been under special orders to engage in propaganda directed at the People's Republic. This, in itself, is of interest because it reveals the seriousness with which the KGB regards the China question and the importance it sees in assigning a top agent to that field.

The concentration of Louis on Chinese topics should be placed in another context as well. It accompanies an extraordinary outpouring of Soviet materials dealing with China in the past decade. In the course of a year it is now not uncommon for Moscow to publish twenty to thirty separate works, some pure propaganda, some a mixture of scholarship and propaganda, and some genuine scholarship, in the Chinese field. The expansion of publication has been enormous and is growing. The bulk of these contributions is devoted to attacks on China policy, "revelations" about Mao Tse-tung (quite often of the same genre as Louis' book, that is, compilations of fact, half-fact, and total fiction), memoirs of Soviet diplomats, correspondents and military personnel who have served in China, and the like.

Thus, in Soviet terms, the Louis book is not unique. It is unusual, however, in being designed for the Western market, having been written in English, and having been composed for sale abroad. Only one other book in the propaganda productions mentioned above, the so-called Vladimirov diaries, a memoir of a Soviet correspondent stationed in Yenan during World War II, had been published in the United States. (Many of the Soviet propaganda works, however, are published in English and other languages in Moscow.) The Vladimirov memoir is based on a genuine document but is demonstrably twisted and spiced with anti-Mao tidbits which have been stuffed in to meet Soviet propaganda objectives.

The Louis book is something quite different and, in a sense, much more important for he has not bothered with minor falsifications. Instead, he has attempted to construct The Big Lie.

It is quite impossible in a brief analysis to deal with every point in Louis' topsy-turvy thesis but, perhaps, nowhere is his argument more interesting than in the case of the Manchu and Manchuria. Here he offers the novel argument that once the Manchu dynasty seized the throne of China (as had not a few nomadic warriors before them) they proceeded systematically to destroy their own people and sinefy Manchuria until today hardly a trace of them remains. Despite their disappearance he argues that they constitute a hotbed of anti-Han hatred and he hints that the Soviet Union may feel compelled to undertake a "liberating mission" in behalf of the Manchu as well as the Tibetans, the Mongols, the Uighurs, and other minorities which he repeatedly stresses now occupy more than 60 percent of the territory of the People's Republic of China. He neglects to mention that all of China's minorities put together constitute only about 5 percent of her population. (In contrast, in the Soviet Union "minority" populations now constitute about 53 percent of the total and the Great Russian Slavs are a true minority within their own country.)

What is interesting about Louis' argument about Manchuria is not its speciousness but that he makes it at all and that he bases himself, in substantial measure, not on contemporary data but upon the observations of scholars and diplomats of the czarist era, particularly those in the reign of Nicholas II, that is, the last years of the nineteenth and early twentieth centuries. This was a time of extreme intrigue by the Russians who were seeking by war, subversion, staged frontier incidents, and bribery of high Chinese officials to detach from the dying Chinese Empire not only Manchuria but Outer Mongolia, Korea, and even north China. They were set back in these aspirations by the Japanese in the Russo-Japanese war of 1904–1905. But Russia never gave them up. She continued to control, for example, the Chinese Eastern Railroad (really a Chinese branch of the Trans-Siberian) down to the 1930s when she had to relinquish it under Japanese pressure.

All of this historical background which reveals the continuity of Russian territorial expansionism in the Far East is absent or lightly passed over in Louis' account. Instead of the reality of two hundred years of consistent Russian expansion at the expense of China he presents a picture of a consistently expansionist, exploitative China.

In the last days of World War II Stalin hastened to make good his Yalta pledge to attack Japan and blitzed the Japanese forces in Manchuria and Korea. He did his best to recover most of the territory which the czar's inept policy had lost in 1905, including the Kuriles, Sakhalin Island, and the northern half of Korea. The Russians reasserted their special rights in Manchuria, including the use of the naval bases of Port Arthur and Dairen and the Chinese Eastern Railroad.

Before withdrawing from Manchuria the Red Army looted the industries and their withdrawal gave an advantage not to the Chinese Communists but to the Nationalists under Chiang Kai-shek. Indeed, Stalin warned Mao Tse-tung not to try to best Chiang in a civil war but to enter a coalition government with Chiang Kai-shek in a subordinate role. Mao rejected Stalin's proposals and went on to win the civil war and come into power himself. Not a whiff of this is to be found in Louis' book.

Even before Mao Tse-tung proclaimed the establishment of the People's Republic in Peking on October 1, 1949, Stalin had invited to Moscow Kao Kang, the Chinese Communist Commissar who controlled what was then called the Autonomous Manchurian Region. Kao Kang and Stalin in June of 1949 signed an independent treaty of mutual assistance.

Later, after Stalin's death, the Peking regime charged that Kao Kang had been plotting with Russia (the precise details were not spelled out because Russia and China were still nominal friends) to make Manchuria independent of China. Kao Kang committed suicide before he could be brought to trial. Louis presents Kao Kang as a martyr to Mao's "anti-Manchurian" chauvinism.

There exists evidence that Stalin provoked the Korean War in furtherance of a complex plot which had as its objective the downfall of Mao Tse-tung and the final achievement of czarist Russia's ancient dream of hegemony over Manchuria, Korea, and north China with a weak regime in power in Peking which could easily be intimidated and blackmailed by a powerful Russia.

This, too, is absent from Louis' work.

Russian ambitions had never been limited to northeast Asia. Throughout the nineteenth century and the opening of the twentieth the Russians nibbled away at what might be called the "soft underbelly" of China. She occupied most of the desert satrapies of Middle Asia which had always paid tribute to the Chinese emperor. These constitute the contemporary Soviet republics of Tadzhikistan, Uzbekistan, much of Kazakhstan, and Kirgizia. She plotted to detach China's sprawling westernmost province of Sinkiang and machinations to this end continued to the time of Chiang Kai-shek's withdrawal from mainland China in 1949 and later.

Tibet was the object of constant struggle between Great Britain and imperial Russia and was saved as an entity within the Chinese Empire only because the two great powers finally recognized a de facto stalemate. Outer Mongolia had been by 1900 under Chinese sovereignty for several hundred years. The Mongols, an independent but increasingly enfeebled race, were hardly happy about this but not strong enough to win freedom. The czar's agents plotted endlessly to win over Mongolia. Finally, in 1911 at the time of the overthrow of the Chinese Empire and the establishment of the first republic under Sun Yat-sen the Russians succeeded and Outer Mongolia became a Russian protectorate. So it is today, although nominally independent. China has never accepted this fait accompli although the People's Republic does maintain attenuated diplomatic relations with Mongolia. Chiang Kai-shek was compelled by World War I diplomacy to acquiesce in Mongol independence but quickly withdrew his agreement once the war had ended.

These vast territorial claims and counterclaims lie in the background of Louis' work. China contends that the whole of the Soviet's eastern marches, all of Siberia east of Baikal, the Maritime Provinces, and Central Asia are Chinese territories taken by Russia by force.

Thus, in a real sense, Louis' arguments about the supposed Chinese minorities and his concern over their "rights" are a kind of crooked reverse image of reality. He paints a picture of an aggressive China and uses it to camouflage the historical pattern of Russian aggression.

This is not an easy case to make and when we examine Louis' argument about Manchuria we find him handling facts like a pretzel bender.

He begins by saying that sinologists are "heatedly debating whether or not the Manchu nation and statehood exists at all." If any such debate is going on it must be confined to a small closed room in Moscow. You will find no academic articles, no great symposia on that subject anywhere. Nor is it surprising that Louis quotes not a single Russian sinologist in support of his contention that a "debate" is in progress. The question of whether a Manchu state exists is not a dead question. It is not even a question. A few pages further Louis concedes that most specialists, including Russians, agree that Manchuria ceased to exist as a national entity in the eighteenth or nineteenth centuries. But almost immediately he is talking of the Japanese in the 1930s "exploiting local sentiments for independence" and advances the thesis that the Chinese (Han) warlord Chang Tso-lin was a Manchu nationalist. He describes in warm terms the Japanese occupation of Manchuria and the puppet "Emperor of Manchukuo," Henry Pu-yi, and points out that Soviet Russia recognized Manchukuo, permitting it to maintain consulates in the Siberian cities of Blagoveshchensk and Chita, the only nation outside Japan to accord such recognition.

He says that Henry Pu-yi was arrested by the Russians but neglects to mention that this occurred during the Soviet blitz of Manchuria in August 1945 nor that the putative emperor was turned over to the Communist Chinese and permitted to live out his life, peacefully and uneventfully, as a gardener at the palace he once occupied in Peking.

He makes the curious assertion that Manchuria was supposed to become independent after the Allied victory over Japan—a pledge which is not to be found in the Big Three deliberations nor those between the Big Three and Chiang Kai-shek.

Louis presents a portrait of Stalin wishing to see a strong China as an outpost of Soviet influence in the Far East at the end of World War II. But if this was Stalin's objective he went at it in a most curious way—trying to subordinate Mao to Chiang Kai-shek and reasserting Soviet influence in areas which czarist Russia had long coveted.

Louis suggests Stalin wanted powerful Communist states in India and Indonesia to balance off against a strong and rival Communist state in China.

If this was Stalin's aim, once again, the record does not show him moving to achieve it. Soviet policy in both India and Indonesia was almost totally inoperative until *after* Stalin's death. Stalin was hostile to India, regarded the Indian independence movement as a British trick and Gandhi as a British puppet. He had little or nothing to do with India and distrusted the Indian Communist party.

Louis suggests that the India–China war was motivated by Mao Tse-tung's desire to destroy the Indian Communist party. But contemporary historical research has established that the Chinese, far from being aggressors in the conflict, made every effort to avoid it. The Soviets, under Khrushchev, showed no interest in the Indian Communists, strongly supported the Nehru government (as Brezhnev did Madame Gandhi) and refused to support the Chinese, openly siding with Nehru. This widened even further the breach between the big Communist states. Louis suggests the Chinese in some way manipulated events in Indonesia to produce the fall of Sukarno and the ensuing massacre of hundreds of thousands of Indonesians of Chinese ethnic origin. Historical record shows, to the contrary, that the Chinese and Soviet Communist parties both engaged in deep and complex intrigues. The Russians wanted a Communist regime favorable to Moscow, the Chinese one favorable to Peking; and the Chinese came very close to achieving this objective.

Louis advances a remarkable suggestion: that the joint operation of the Chinese Nationals and Communists during and just before World War II against the Japanese and their puppets in north China and Manchuria was in reality a chauvinistic Chinese effort to wipe out the remnants of the Manchu race. "The much vaunted anti-Japanese struggle in Manchuria was therefore in effect," Louis says, "an anti-Manchurian struggle." It would be difficult to stand truth on its head more spectacularly.

He may be more revealing than he intends in picturing Kao Kang, the leader of the quasi-independent Manchurian Autonomous regime in 1949 as seeking to achieve "some kind of independent administrative and political unity." This is exactly what Peking charged that Kao Kang was plotting with Stalin. One cannot take Louis' assertions as lending great weight to the theory of a Kao Kang—Stalin plot but, as far as it goes, it is evidence in support of this conspiratorial reading.

Louis' analysis of Outer and Inner Mongolia relationships is as tendentious as that of Manchuria. He suggests, for example, that the rebuilding of the tomb of Genghis Khan in Inner Mongolia is an example of Mongol chauvinism in Inner Mongolia in defiance of the Chinese. In fact, China's willingness to permit the existence of a virtual Genghis Khan cult has been a strong talking point for China and Inner Mongolia against Russian-dominated Outer Mongolia.

Genghis Khan is the hero of all Mongols, Inner, Outer, Buryat, Kalmyk. He is the one authentic Mongol hero and symbol of Mongol nationalism. But to the Russians he is the symbol of the greatest catastrophe ever to befall the Slav nation—the devastating conquest of Russia by Genghis Khan and his Golden Horde in the late thirteenth century. The Mongols held sway in Russia for nearly three hundred years and their very name raises the hair on the back of Russian necks. Genghis Khan is hated by patriotic Russians as though the conquest had occurred only yesterday. In propaganda against China they invoke the memory of the Mongols. Even the liberal poet Yevgeny Yevtushenko evoked this image in a poem against the Chinese published in *Pravda* at the time of the 1969 Sino-Soviet crisis.

The Russians have never permitted their wards in Outer Mongolia to glorify Genghis Khan. He is not seen as a positive national leader. He is seen as the scourge of the earth. But in Inner Mongolia the Chinese have no such scruples. They encourage the Mongols to do what comes naturally—erect statues, paint pictures, publish poems about Genghis Khan. This has long been known in Outer Mongolia. In fact until the 1960s Outer Mongols often visited Inner Mongolia and one of the great attractions was the shrine of Genghis Khan—plus books, magazines, and newspapers printed in the old Mongol script (Tibetan) instead of the bastardized Cyrillic imposed upon Outer Mongolia by the Soviet "advisors."

It would be tedious to set straight all the convoluted "facts" which Louis has strung together about the two Mongolias. But it is not tedious to note his major premise. He declares that at the end of World War II Stalin prevented Outer Mongolia from absorbing Inner Mongolia and creating a Greater Mongolia. He does not explain that Stalin had put his bet on Chiang Kai-shek and had just persuaded Chiang reluctantly to recognize the "independence" of Outer Mongolia.

Up to now, says Louis, Prime Minister Tsedenbal of the Mongolian Peoples' Republic (far more canny and sensible in his political thinking than Louis) has refused to raise the question of a "divided" Mongolia, taking the position that "Inner Mongolia is within the boundaries of another socialist country," that is, China. Louis might have added that Buryatia, formerly called Buryat-Mongolia, another Mongol enclave, is within the boundaries of another socialist country (the USSR).

However, Louis feels that Tsedenbal's argument no longer holds good because in Moscow China is no longer considered a "member of the socialist camp" and therefore Mongol leaders "who usually toe the Soviet line" will no doubt "correct their attitude."

He advances an ingenious idea. Why not invite the Dalai Lama to leave India and take up residence in Mongolia? This would solve two problems with one shot. It would create an irresistible demand on the part of Mongols in China to join their coreligionists in Outer Mongolia and it would give powerful momentum to the movement to free Tibet from Chinese clutches.

The world being what it is there seems little likelihood that this suggestion will be taken up. But if it is an example of the schemes now being brainstormed within the KGB that organization would seem to have acquired the kind of irresponsible characteristics that led the CIA to try to put poison in Castro's boots in order to make his beard fall out.

What is important to keep in mind is that the Dalai Lama idea could not spring full-blown from Louis' forehead. It had to be implanted there and cleared for publication by the men for whom he works.

Louis' potted history of China's western regions, the desert and mountain territory of Sinkiang is, as might be expected, consistent with his accounts of the other Chinese border regions. That is, he seeks to establish the proposition that China is suppressing a large ethnic minority in contrast to a warm and friendly Soviet approach to these people. His résumé falls short of revealing the consistent Russian intrigues and power plays which had as their objective the detachment of the area from China, a program that Stalin was able to continue even after 1949 when he compelled Mao Tse-tung to agree to the establishment of joint Soviet–Chinese mining, oil, and air transport enterprises in Sinkiang. Only Stalin's death and the rise of Khrushchev brought the liquidation of these enterprises in which Moscow held a controlling 51 percent of the stock.

The picture painted by Louis of "a people enchained" within China bears a monstrous resemblance to the image which so long has characterized Russia. In czarist days Russia was known as "the prison house of nations." The image has changed somewhat today but there are still many who contend that given a substantial shock the USSR would break apart. In fact, this is the thesis of Amalrik in his well-known book: *Will Russia Survive After 1984?* Alexander Solzhenitsyn ardently advocates the disssolution of the union and the divorce of the Great Slavs, that is the Russians, from the non-Slav nationalities, the Baltic peoples, the Caucasian peoples, and the Central Asian peoples.

This is the counterimage of the goal which Louis seeks for China and he predicts that the minority peoples will fight their way out of China's grasp with, as he constantly hints, the aid of the Soviet Union.

Louis has one more string to his bow. Not only does he picture China sitting on the back of repressed minorities but also he sees Peking itching to conquer the Soviet Maritime Provinces, eastern Siberia, and Central Asia.

He considers that the present policy of the People's Republic is synonymous with that of nineteenth-century China when a Chinese representative declared that "All that lies to the West of Lake Baikal is part of Russia and all that lies to the East is part of China." Whether that was the actual view of the last Ching dynasty is another point. It is true that the Chinese have repeatedly declared that the Russians possess something like a million square miles of territory once held under sway of the Chinese Empire. But the Chinese have also said that they realize it is too late to get all of this back.

Louis pictures Mao as trying to provoke world war between Russia and the United States in order to realize his territorial aspirations against the USSR, hoping that the two great nuclear powers would destroy each other to China's benefit.

That strategy will not work, he declares, because the Soviet Union will move with cold calculation to meet the threat of Chinese aggression and will not hesitate to launch military action against the People's Republic.

"This is all the more true since time is working in China's favor," Louis adds. And here he has reached the theme and purpose of his volume: to lay a foundation, however dubious it may be, on which the Soviet-Union could justify launching an attack on the People's Republic, a preemptive strike to keep China from seizing Soviet territory and, at the same time, to carry out "a liberating mission" in favor of oppressed minority peoples within China.

Louis sees panic sweeping China's border and minority areas if war or rumor of war arises. This has happened before, he argues, and would happen again.

He offers two enigmatic bits of information. There exists in Siberia, he reports, a kind of Siberia-first lobby which wishes to build up a Siberia-oriented economy, trading more widely with East Asia and the Pacific and more independent of Moscow's apron strings. Moscow has inhibited such development by fears of too much local autonomy and possibly because of fear of war with China. In the five Soviet Central Asia republics, he says, there is a strong unification movement. The republics would like to form a Central Asian Soviet Republic which might be the basis for a greater Asian federation ultimately including within the Soviet Union such areas as Sinkiang and possibly Mongolia.

The relationship of the Siberian and Central Asian movements to the Sino-Soviet quarrel is not made clear by Louis but obviously a Soviet Central Asian Republic might possess a strong attractive power for related minorities beyond the Soviet frontier.

Louis halts short of predicting war between Russia and China. But he accuses the Chinese of genocide, talks about compelling the Chinese to answer before the United Nations and world public opinion, and, then, in a typically left-handed fashion, reverts to what he calls an early idea of Lenin's for setting up a system of buffer states around China, a kind of *cordon sanitaire*. Just as the Soviet is protected on its western frontier with Europe by satellite states so it would be protected on the east by a network of Manchuria (or would they revive the name Manchukuo?), greater Mongolia, Free Tibet under the Dalai

Lama, an independent Uighuria or whatever name the Russians might give to the Sinkiang vastness.

It seems like poppycock—a perverse assortment of untruths, half truths, and plain lies but there it is. As the Russians say paper will take anything you put on it. All this, ridiculous as it may sound, is not ridiculous. It has a serious purpose. It is designed to disorient our thinking about Russia and China, to confuse American ideas about the Soviet–Chinese clash, to alarm and disturb the Chinese, to put them off balance, and ultimately, if need be, to serve as a chapbook for Moscow propagandists to quote when, as, and if the Kremlin deems the moment ripe for war with China. That moment may never come. But as Chekhov once said if a gun is hanging on the wall in the first act of a play it is certain to go off before the end of the third.

What Louis has sketched is the design of a Russian blunderbuss. It is worthy of careful study because the Sino-Soviet quarrel is basic; one of the most dangerous in the world and what Louis accomplishes is to give it a pseudohistorical, pseudopolitical framework to justify whatever aggression the Kremlin decides upon.

If this scenario seems to emanate a more than paranoid aroma that is only because the quarrel between the two countries is no longer being fought with words.

# CONTENTS

xix

# FOREWORD

China's role in the modern world should be evaluated by the weight it carries in present-day international affairs. Of far more significance is the China of tomorrow. For that matter, as a political phenomenon, such a projection of the future onto the present is not so very unusual. If it is true that there are countries whose international stature today is largely derived from memories of their great past, why should the reverse dependence not be equally valid, provided of course that the great future which is overshadowing the present eventually materializes? In respect to China this condition is causing the greatest doubts.

The fact is that modern China has inherited from the Manchu Empire not only its territory, equal to the size of Europe, but also a hereditary disease which may well prove fatal for the body politic. Powerful centrifugal forces are at work tending to wrest vast national territories away from China. These lands, whose continued presence within the modern boundaries of China is much less than certain, make up over half its total area. When and if these lands finally fall away will be the culmination of a long process.

Oswald Spengler has likened civilizations to flowers which have their period of full bloom, then just as inexorably fall, wither, and die. In its heyday the Chinese Empire was surrounded by a cluster of colonies, like the petals of a flower. But as time went on the petals began to fall away one after another. Burma fell away, then Annam. Nepal and Korea became independent. They were followed by Outer Mongolia and Tibet.[1]

> The rose has lost its first petal
> To the winds of spring;
> So the time is not far distant
> When the last will also fall.

Thus wrote Rabindranath Tagore and poetical prophecies have been known to become political ones.

It certainly looks as if the key to the future of China is to be found in the future of its outlying areas with their non-Chinese (i.e., non-Han) population.[2]

As soon as the last of these colonial petals (of what once was the Manchu Empire) falls away, the remainder will make up barely 40 percent of China's present territory. But if this is indeed the future toward which China is moving with fatal inexorability, we must inevitably alter our assessment of present-day China.

In working on this book, I have traveled the entire length of the Soviet-Chinese border—from the Pacific to the Pamirs. My observations and encounters in the course of these travels have helped me to sum up my earlier reflections and conclusions.

---

[1] After four decades of independence Tibet was reoccupied by China in 1951.
[2] Hereafter I shall often refer to the Chinese people (the country's largest ethnic group) as the Han people to avoid confusion with "Chinese people" meaning inhabitants of China or members of a political unit.—V.L.

# THE COMING
# DECLINE OF
# THE CHINESE
# EMPIRE

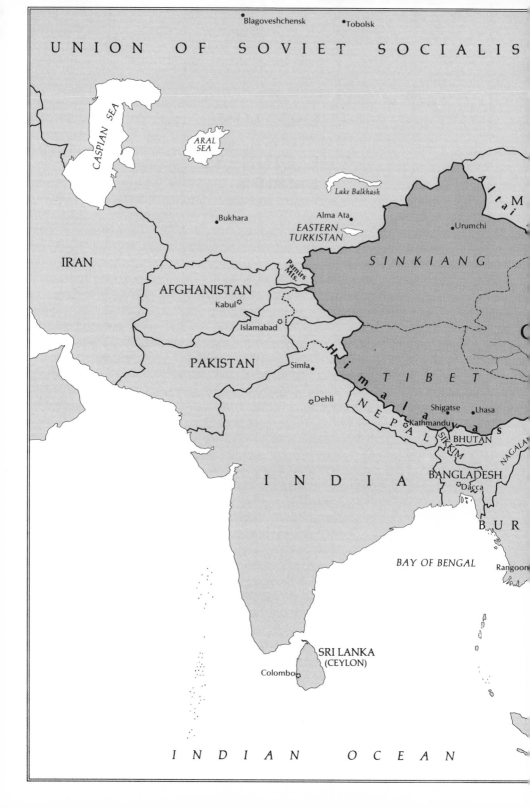

# PART I

# 1

# MANCHURIA: A COUNTRY THAT IS NOT

## *The Manchu Dispute*

In the long list of accusations which are leveled against the "gang of four" in China, their crimes and errors in carrying out the nationalities policy are among the most important. All the minority districts are mentioned in this connection with the sole exception of Manchuria. The same holds true when the Chinese leaders speak of achievements in this field; again the only minority that is not mentioned is the Manchurian.

Many years of China-watching have taught me that every word uttered by Chinese officials, as well as everything passed over in silence, is as full of covert meaning as a hieroglyph. So the Manchurian problem contains much more than might at first appear—and much that is tragic.

Why is this people, numbering about three million and with a history of its own going back for many more centuries than most Western states, doomed not only to be passed over in silence but in fact to be relegated to what amounts to nonexistence? The answer can be given in a single sentence: What has befallen Manchuria and its people is a model solution to the nationalities problem as it is understood in China. Present-day Chinese leaders regard the "solution of the Manchurian problem" as the prototype for resolving the mosaic of nationalities which has always haunted China.

To understand how the model works, we must start with history—indeed with ancient history—in the third century B.C.

In the third century B.C. "the Emperor Ch'in, the First Emperor of the Ch'in dynasty, built the Great Wall of China, and the Han dynasty erected a barrier which separated the inner world from the external." Thus was the building of the Great Wall described in the Chinese classic *Hou Han-shu (Later History of the Han)*. Manchuria, which belonged to the outside world, was left outside the Wall. Several centuries later the Great Wall failed to protect China from the Manchu invasion—later still it proved just as powerless to save the Manchus themselves from China.

In 1644 "the Manchus defeated the Chinese, and China became a part of the Manchu Empire." The Manchu army took Peking and the Manchu emperors became the rulers of China. For the next three centuries the language spoken in the imperial palaces at Peking was that of the Manchu.

In contrast to most other historical cases of this kind, however, the traditional relationships of victor and vanquished assumed a rather paradoxical form. The formal incorporation of China into Manchuria in effect became the incorporation of Manchuria into China because the military victory was not followed by an ethnical, linguistical, or cultural victory. Moreover, after the establishment of Manchu rule in China the vanquished began to devour the victors and, as *Bol'shaia Sovietskaia Entsiklopediia (Great Soviet Encyclopedia)* puts it, "there began the assimilation of Manchu culture and the loss by the Manchus of their native tongue."

The result is that today, three centuries after the Manchu people had the misfortune to defeat "the great Han people," sinologists are heatedly debating whether or not the Manchu nation and statehood exists at all. According to the advocates of Manchu statehood, Manchuria has its own history and national traditions which are many thousands of years old. Geographically, ethnically, and culturally, as well as historically, Manchuria is clearly distinct from China. Prior to 1644, when the Manchu occupied Peking, "the two countries had no bonds between them and lived in a state of periodic military conflict."

Characteristically, when the first Russian missions traveled to China through Manchuria in the sixteenth and seventeenth centuries, the Manchu rulers invariably did their utmost to block such contacts. This is an indication not only of the nature of the relations that existed between the two countries, Manchuria and China, but also of the extent of Manchuria's influence and authority in international relations.

At no time in Manchu history did the Chinese administration extend its influence beyond a very small area in the lower reaches of the Liao River, while the whole of China was under Manchu rule for a full three hundred years. Throughout the entire period of Manchu domination in China, Manchuria proper continued to be governed directly by a Manchu administration.

Manchuria's neighbors have likewise always regarded Manchuria as an isolated national entity, very distinct from China proper. Thus, most historical references to the seizure of the Russian outpost of Albazin in the spring of 1685 emphasize that it was captured by a Manchu force. The boundary that was drawn there in 1869 was also viewed by the Russians as a boundary with Manchuria, not China. For centuries the Chinese themselves also treated their neighbor Manchuria as foreign territory inhabited by "northern barbarians."

So until a certain period in history the existence of the Manchu and Manchuria was never called into question. But for some time now Chinese authors have been doing just that—and, what is more, asserting that the Manchu do not exist and never have existed. "The so called 'Manchus,'" one Chinese author has written, "do not constitute any 'race' in the ethnical sense, as many people tend to believe." [1] It is further alleged that "the history of Manchuria is, of course, but a part of Chinese history."

Denial of the Manchu's existence as a nation is to be found in the works of many Chinese authors, including those loyal to the present Chinese regime. One example is the work by Sun Tse, *The Guerrilla Struggle in Manchuria*, where the events described are regarded as a

---

[1] From *Manchuria in History: A Summary* by Li Chi, published in Peiping, 1932, pp. 1-2.

struggle by the Chinese against the Japanese on the indigenously Chinese territory of the "fictitious state of Manchukuo." As for the history or geography of Manchuria, they are referred to ironically, if at all.

It is thereby alleged that the Manchu as a nation do not exist—and never did.

These attempts to reshape history have never been an abstract or academic exercise. The methods applied have been twofold: the military extermination of the Manchu and the mass settlement of Chinese immigrants in the territory.

Evidence of the first method was found as far back as 1692 by a Russian ambassador, Ides Izbrantes, when he traveled to Peking. He recorded his impressions of several devastated and deserted Manchu towns. "After another six days of traveling through hilly terrain, again without encountering a single dwelling, we reached another large ancient and deserted town, Daimingcheng, protected by a rectangular wall and strong bastions. There were two towers, one very tall, the other smaller, its broad octangular facade made of brick. At a height of about ten sazhens [70 feet/21 meters] above the ground we could see stones on which eight rows of various images had been carved."

Further on in the envoy's diary we find a description of another dead city. "On one side the city was protected by earthen fortifications, with bastions of extraordinary height and size, but there were only four entrances in the form of gates through which vast numbers of rabbits were scampering into the big city to feast on the grass. There was hardly a single living soul in the city. The Chinese tell us that many centuries ago, during the rule of the Tatar king, Uzhai Khan, the place was conquered by the Chinese Bogdo Khan, and the Tatars were chased away. It seems to me that the city is more than one German mile in circumference."

Time and again as he was making his way to the Great Wall through Manchuria, the ambassador came across towns that had been abandoned by the Manchu. "After four days of travelling," he recalled, "we reached the old and deserted town of Burgankoton, or City of Idols. it has been given that name because no one has lived in it since ancient times."

These were all traces of efforts to deny the existence of the Manchu as a nation by force of arms. The other aspect of the same policy of denying their existence was, as already mentioned, the mass resettlement of Chinese immigrants in Manchuria.

Once seated upon the Dragon Throne in Peking, the Manchu found themselves face to face with a dilemma. On the one hand, as Manchu, they were supposed to protect their nation from assimilation by the Han Chinese. On the other, as emperors of China, they were supposed to be interested in such assimilation. And so the ultimate destiny of the Manchu nation was in the hands of successive emperors and it depended on whether they regarded themselves primarily as Manchu or as exponents of the interests of the Han people. Up to 1878 the Chinese emperors of the Manchu, or Ching, dynasty were first and foremost Manchu.

Until that year they did their utmost to save their country from being ethnically, culturally, and linguistically absorbed by China. Thus, the earliest Manchu emperors of China issued edicts proscribing the settlement of Han Chinese in Manchuria. One such edict forbade Chinese women to travel beyond the Great Wall. This compelled those Chinese men who went to Manchuria as seasonal workers to return home after the end of the farming season.

The Manchu emperors were not the first to become aware of the great power of the "call of sex." Far back in history, in fording the Rhone River during his Roman campaign, Hannibal encountered a situation which required him to display qualities other than the traditional gallantry of the military leader. The elephants, which were the main strike force of his army, dug in their heels and would not cross the river. Hannibal then ordered a raft to be made on which a cow elephant was carried to the other bank. Seeing their sweetheart on the other side, the elephants threw themselves into the water and several minutes later were all on the other bank. In Peking the Manchu emperors did the very opposite by preventing the "cow elephant" from going to the other side.

While some measures were meant to impede the settlement of Chinese in Manchuria, others were aimed at keeping the Manchu themselves inside Manchuria. Practically every Manchu adult was paid something like a life pension by the imperial government. But on one condition: The pension was only paid as long as he did not leave his own country. Anyone leaving Manchuria forfeited his pension at the same time.

Finally, there was a third set of measures designed to save the Manchu as a nation. Under the Ching dynasty the language of the Manchu was made the official language of the Chinese Empire. All formal documents in China—and also in Mongolia and partially in Korea—had to be written in the Manchu language. To qualify for a government post, officials had to take an examination in the Manchu language. By 1910 it had been introduced as a separate and obligatory subject in Peking schools. By 1912 a Manchu newspaper was being printed. But these were no more than final convulsive and futile efforts.

Some of the efforts made to preserve certain attributes of Manchu culture did yield results. For instance, many Chinese adopted the Manchu style of dress. The traditional image of the Chinese man with the inevitable pigtail also came to China from Manchuria. The pigtail derived from the desire to look like a horse. To increase the similarity the Manchu not only grew pigtails, symbol of the horse's tail, they also shaved their foreheads to elongate their faces. Observance of this custom signified loyalty to the Manchu rulers. Noncompliance meant the absence of loyalty. And since disloyalty has always been a punishable offense all over the world, it was certainly not for China to prove the exception. "We are very strict about our pigtail," the Russian traveler Sergei Runin was told in Manchuria. "If someone should cut off his pigtail, after the pigtail the Chian Chun (local governor) will cut off his head."

Thus, some of the external attributes of Manchu influence were quite vigorously enforced—to the point of beheading would-be dissidents. Not for nothing did Sun Yat-sen exhort the Chinese "to overcome the Manchu influence and to develop the Han."

We have a curious situation here—at least for the Western mentality. On the one hand, there is a piece of a land called Manchuria. There is a Manchu language with its own distinctive alphabet. There is ample evidence of the enduring influence of Manchu culture on the Chinese which prompted Sun Yat-sen to utter the words quoted above. On the other hand, the Chinese are now going out of their way to assert that "the so-called Manchus" simply do not exist and never did.

Which of these two mutually exclusive statements should one accept?

Strange as it may seem, they are both true to a certain extent. To understand this paradox, common enough in Chinese history, one must turn to the past to those days when the first Chinese settlers appeared in Manchuria.

## The Yellow Wave From the South

The Chinese penetration of Manchuria began long before the ban was formally lifted in 1878. This did not mean the establishment of a laissez-faire system, but of a very intensive resettlement policy. "Instead of prohibitive measures," the Russian scholar D.A. Davydov writes, "the Chinese government, sacrificing the home country of its reigning dynasty in the national interests, elaborates a series of projects to encourage the resettlement of Manchuria from China proper."

Two years after permission to settle in Manchuria was officially given, the central government instituted a special Colonisation Office for this purpose. The Colonisation Office got down to business with an alacrity that was in marked contrast to the traditional portrayal of oriental sluggishness. Firstly, it laid down that all officials in Manchuria failing to resettle 25,000 people from China proper in their area were to be sacked. At the same time the recruitment of potential resettlers was started throughout China. Those who agreed to emigrate to Manchuria were given loans and provided with guides who accompanied them to their final destination. The head of the family traveled at half price; the other members of the family—and in China they are very numerous—were transported free of charge. Furthermore, in contrast to the rest of China, only a part of his plot of land was taxed. Thus a concerted effort was made to entice as many Han Chinese as possible to resettle in Manchuria—or as it now came to be called, Tung Pei, meaning Northeast. This change of names, which obliterated the name of the people from the map, is in itself quite significant.

It is not surprising that the upshot of all these measures was a massive migration of Chinese to the north. As the Russian traveler Dobrolovsky wrote later, "in the last three or four years (1900–1904) thousands of new Chinese settlements have appeared throughout the province of Heilungkiang." This process was observed by another Russian author, A. Kokhanovsky. "In my visits to Manchuria," he wrote, "in 1900–1902 as a doctor, I would frequently find new villages where there had been nothing but steppe land at the time of my previous visit." D.A. Davydov described the appearance of new Chinese settlements in Manchuria. The first peasant house (fanza) would be built somewhere in the steppe. Then "others would be erected around this first fanza—perhaps for relatives or friends—and thus an entire village would be founded. In my travels I came across many such solitary fanzas housing one family, or sometimes they would be empty—probably until the arrival of a representative of the family."

Important in Manchuria's sinification was the fact that until the overthrow of the Ching dynasty the territory was the arena of a largely unpublicized struggle between two giants, the Russian Empire and China. In true European style Russia laid its stakes on economic inroads—concessions, banks, railways, and the like—while the Chinese government pinned its hopes on the resettlers—that human flood which was supposed to engulf and swamp all those banks, concessions, and railways brought in from without.

But this confrontation turned out to be a highly contradictory process. The masses of Chinese shipped north by the Peking government to counteract the Russian influence actually helped to increase that influence for this was the cheap manpower that is so essential for any thriving enterprise.

So in the same way that the Russians were promoting the success of the Chinese policy the Chinese were unwillingly helping the Russians. As A. Kokhanovsky wrote at the time in his book *Resettlement in China and Our Far Eastern Borderland*, "Our commercial and industrial undertakings along the borders, both on our side and on the Chinese side, rendered great assistance in the Chinese resettlement, and especially helpful to China was our Manchurian railroad, which at its own expense assembled Chinese from various provinces, carrying them by sea and over land, and giving them almost unlimited pay at the building sites, ... and which shifted the centre of life from Blagoveshchensk to Harbin." The same belief that the penetration of Russian capital increased the influx of immigrants will be found in the works of other Russian authors. In this somewhat curious struggle between two methods of expansion—the European and the Asian—it was the Asian method that carried the day. The principle of *wu-shou-li-chuan*, that is, "return of rights and privileges," tacitly applied by the Chinese government of Manchuria, triumphed.

As time went on, the resettlement wave from China welled higher and higher. The steadily rising number of Chinese immigrants is shown by these figures:

| YEAR | HAN IMMIGRANTS |
|------|----------------|
| 1923 | 341,638 |
| 1924 | 384,730 |
| 1925 | 472,978 |
| 1926 | 566,725 |
| 1927 | 1,050,828 |
| 1928 | 1,089,000 |

This population increase gave the entire country an entirely new look. The indigenous population was soon reduced to an exotic minority in their own land. At the turn of the century—even in Manchuria itself—the Manchu language began falling into disuse. "At present," wrote the Russian scholar M.I. Suvirov, "only the Tatar tribes in the remote areas of Heilungkiang and Kirin provinces use it." By 1900 Han Chinese acounted for about 80 percent of Manchuria's population. Today the figure is as high as 90 percent and in a total population of 30 million those who speak Manchu total no more than 100,000. The rest, as stated in Soviet journal *Sovietskaya Etnografia (Soviet Ethnography),* "were assimilated and have lost their distinctive features" under the influence of Chinese culture. Thus, of the total number of people who identified themselves as Manchu in the census of 1953, only 4 percent knew their native language; the rest probably continued to call themselves Manchu from a sense of residual ethnic pride. The Manchu can be divided into those who call themselves Manchu but no longer know their language and those who have a slight knowledge of it but no longer regard themselves as Manchu. This would seem to indicate various phases of assimilation and loss of national identity. As long ago as 1928, the Russian scholar E.E.

Yashkov wrote that in Manchuria the local peasantry "seems in general to be completely uniform and quite sinified. Only in some of the outlying districts can one encounter small groups of Manchus or other natives who have retained some of their distinctive characteristics."

This process of intensive assimilation which the Chinese resettlers always carried with them has been noted by many authors. One such observation belongs to Abbot Huke. He visited southern Manchuria in the 1840s at the very time when some of the land in the area was being set aside for sale to the Chinese immigrants. "The Chinese," the abbot wrote, "swooped down on the plots like birds of prey, and it took no more than a few years to destroy all that could in the least degree recall memories of their former owners." This was a local rehearsal for what later became the fate of an entire nation. The abbot pointed out that in Manchuria he could not escape the impression that he was not in another country but merely in one of the provinces of China.

The legend of King Midas, whose touch turned all to gold, comes involuntarily to mind when one thinks of the nations that have been and still are being absorbed by the Han. All that comes into contact with China itself becomes Chinese. The lot of the vanquished and the conquered has never been an enviable one. But as the fate of the Manchu has proved, the lot of the conqueror is sometimes no better. Those who have been conquered by China and those who have themselves conquered China have the same fate in store for them. And that fate is gradual assimilation and extinction.

By this token the Chinese allegations about the Manchu not existing as a nation prove to be only too true. Yielding to the Chinese views on this score, the *Great Soviet Encyclopedia* stated several years ago that the Manchu ceased to exist as a nation in the eighteenth–nineteenth centuries. Actually this happened somewhat later, some two or three generations after 1878. The exact date cannot be established but it is not so very important. The important point is that it did happen. When the Chinese Communists held their famous People's Congress in 1946, they adopted a manifesto calling for "the equality of nationalities: Mongols, Moslems, Koreans." Characteristically, the Manchu were not included in this list of nationalities inhabiting Chinese territory. It was as if they had never existed. The nation simply ceased to be.

## Manchukuo—Ghost or Reality?

The story of the rise and fall of the state of Manchukuo is well known. On February 19, 1932, a declaration was made public in Mukden. The next day it was reprinted in all the leading newspapers of the world. In its first paragraph the declaration, on behalf of the 30-million-strong Manchurian people, proclaimed the establishment of a new state, "on the basis of racial self-determination" and "independence of the Chinese Republic." "The principle of racial equality," the declaration emphasized, "shall be adhered to by Chinese, Manchurian and Mongolian natives, Korean and Japanese inhabitants, and residents of other nationalities in the Manchurian state shall be accorded equal treatment."

As we have seen, however, there were almost no Manchu proper left in Manchuria in 1932: Only one in every 300 inhabitants could speak Manchu. The new state would therefore have become a Manchuria without Manchu if someone had not had the bright idea of declaring all its citizens to be Manchurians: "Fully 97 percent of the total population of Manchuria are Manchurians of varied origins, including Chinese."

For those familiar with the history of this part of the Far East the declaration of Manchuria's independence came as no surprise. There was a certain amount of logic in the event, though it was not the kind of logic that lies on the surface. As much logic, surely, as in the fact that present-day Turkey is situated in an area which used to be the Byzantine Empire. Or that modern Egypt is where ancient Egypt once used to be. It matters little that there is no cultural, linguistic, or ethnic continuity between the Byzantine Greeks and the Turks who overran their country or between the ancient Egyptians and the Arabs who today make their home on the Nile. The important thing is that in some cases states come into being on the basis of nationality, in others on the basis of geography. One example of a state that owes its existence primarily to geography is Great Britain; to this day it has not overcome the ethnic and even linguistic disparity of its various components.

The case of Manchuria is similar. Geographically its center is an isolated plain circled in the north by the Khingan Mountains, separated from the Korean peninsula by the East Manchurian Highlands and from Peking by the rugged Jehol Mountains, long an imperial Manchu hunting area. Manchuria's geographical isolation is in itself a factor prompting it to seek political and state independence quite irrespective of the national identity of the people or peoples who inhabit it. The attempt to bind Manchuria to China by filling it with Chinese proved just as effective as an attempt to bind a jug to a spring with the water jet that is filling it. Instead of being bound to the spring the jug will simply carry away the water that the spring has poured into it. Similarly, instead of binding the territory to China, the 30 million Chinese who filled Manchuria's steppelands found themselves potentially torn away from China.

The only thing the Japanese, who were so active in shaping the destinies of Manchukuo, could do was to try to exploit the already existing tendencies toward independence and secession from China. As early as the beginning of this century D.A. Davydov noted the widespread sentiments in favor of autonomy from China among the local population.

It is not surprising that these sentiments acquired new strength immediately after the collapse of imperial power in Peking. When Chang Tso-lin proclaimed the territory's autonomy in 1922 this was much more than an arbitrary decision by a politician. Even before the declaration of independence Manchuria's autonomy was by no means purely symbolic. The country had its own monetary unit which differed from the Chinese currency. The taxes collected in Manchuria did not flow into the treasury of the central Chinese government but remained in Manchuria. Chang Tso-lin had his own army of 3500 men. At the time of the armed conflict with Soviet Russia, Manchurian troops alone took part which strongly indicates that the incident involved primarily Manchuria, not China as a whole.

Many foreigners visiting Manchuria at the time emphasized this process of drawing away from China, the ultimate aim of which was complete secession and independence. One such visitor, Klaus Menert, pointed out that it was Chang Tso-lin, not Chiang Kai-shek, who in fact governed the territory.

But there were other facts of a more formal nature—this time from the domain of diplomatic practice. The well-known agreements of 1924 with Soviet Russia were signed separately by the central Chinese government and the Manchurian government at Mukden. Though Japan was the only country to have diplomatic relations with Manchukuo, the other great powers nonetheless maintained consular relations with the new state. Considering their reluctance to aggravate their relations with China, this was surely a form of mild recognition. The United States, Great Britain, France, and Italy had consulates in Manchuria. Russia went even further by arranging an exchange of consular officials between Manchuria and the Soviet Union. The flag of the independent Manchurian state was displayed in Blagoveshchensk outside the residence of the Manchurian consul, Hui Kong-chi, and in Chita outside the residence of the consul there, Li Yuan.

Three world powers—Japan, China, and Russia—vied with each other in asserting their influence over Manchuria. China wanted to turn it into one of its provinces, Japan into a protectorate, and Russia into "Yellow Russia." Accordingly, anything or anyone who promoted Manchuria's independence was antagonistic to the aspirations of the three powers and, from the standpoint of their leaders, was to be destroyed. The fate of three successive Manchurian rulers who personified the idea of independence, Chang Tso-lin, his son and heir Chang Hsueh-liang, and the last Manchurian emperor Pu-Yi, illustrates this antagonism.

Chang Tso-lin was killed by the Japanese; Chang Hsueh-liang was imprisoned by the Kuomintang (Chinese Nationalist party's) government of China and Pu-Yi was arrested and spent some time in prison in Russia before he was returned to China. (Ironically enough while still ruler of Manchuria, Pu-Yi had taken pains to learn Russian, as if preparing to meet his fate.)

So China, Japan, and Russia all played a part in ending Manchuria's independence. But the real credit must surely go to China.

In listing the motives that prompted China to display such interest in Manchuria, priority is frequently given to Manchuria's economic potential. Southern Manchuria is indeed fittingly called the Ruhr of the Far East; it accounts for 70 percent of the iron ore, 30 percent of the coal, and 50 percent of the electric power produced by the whole of China.

Yet this admittedly powerful consideration was not China's main argument against parting with Manchuria.

It is easy to see that a truly independent Manchuria (which is exactly what it was supposed to become after the Allied victory over Japan) would have posed a terrible danger for China's unity. The secession of that territory, inhabited as it was by Chinese, would have produced the same effect as the detonation of a bomb. The ensuing explosion would have broken China into pieces. And the pieces themselves were sufficiently isolated both in terms of nationality and past traditions of independent statehood. Though attached to China by the steel shackles of administrative, military, and political power, the peoples of the various minority areas had never identified themselves with the Han people. This applies above all to Inner Mongolia, Sinkiang, Tibet, and other non-Han-populated territories which together make up 60 percent of China's entire land area. For this reason, when China's political future was being decided in the battles between the Communist and the Kuomintang armies somewhere in the central and southern areas, the question of whether China, as such, was to be or not to be was being decided in the north, in Manchuria. The breakaway of Manchuria would have caused the whole of China to collapse like a house of cards and would surely have spelled the end of its existence as a major world power.

This was clearly understood by both the Kuomintang and the Chinese Communists. It was clearly understood by Moscow as well. So each of those three forces—Moscow, the Chinese Communists, and the Kuomintang—was equally interested in preventing this from happening. For the Kuomintang and the Chinese Communists alike the problem involved the very existence of the administrative and political complex which they both associated with their concept of home and country. As for Moscow, Stalin needed the great China as an outpost of Soviet influence in the East although Moscow was even then aware of the potential threat that China could pose for the Soviet leadership within the Communist movement. But Russia believed that before China could attain a sufficient level of economic, industrial, and military development to become a rival of the Soviet Union, the revolutionizing influence of the new China would awaken powerful forces in Asia which would offset the possible Chinese threat. Such forces could indeed have arisen as a result of a Communist victory in India or Indonesia.

Mao Tse-tung must have seen through the Russian designs. What is more, he did his best to prevent the development in Asia of an alternative Communist force that could compete with China. To this end Peking carried out two consecutive maneuvers which for a long time to come removed from its path two potential rivals in the world Communist movement: the Communist parties of both India and Indonesia.

The first blow was struck at the Indian Communists. The Sino-Indian frontier dispute, precipitated by China, looked from the very outset like a piece of political nonsense. The miserable scraps of uninhabitable land to which China laid claim were surely not worth the incalculable moral loss that China sustained by exposing itself to the world in the role of aggressor. It certainly seems hard to imagine that the Chinese leaders, in planning their action, could have failed to foresee the inevitable consequences. And yet they lashed out at India even though their international prestige dropped to its lowest level ever. For the sake of what?

When the dispute was still in the open, the end results were too vague to be predicted. They have become clearer today and we can now speak with greater certainty about the objectives underlying the outwardly senseless actions of the Chinese leaders.

The blow delivered by Peking across the Sino-Indian border was aimed at the Indian Communist party.

In the very first hours of the conflict the Indian Communists found themselves faced with the choice of displaying solidarity either with their bourgeois government or with the Communist party of China. Their sense of international Communist comradeship prevailed. And anyway, every Communist is familiar with the now-canonized words uttered by Lenin that in the event of a conflict between imperialist powers, the Communists of each country must fight for the defeat of their government. So it was only too natural that, as soon as the conflict erupted, the leadership of the Indian Communist party issued a statement laying the blame for aggression on the bourgeois Indian government and declaring solidarity with the Chinese Communists. By this token the Indian Communists became the sole political group in India to support the aggressor who had attacked the country. The Indian public was horrified. India's teeming millions, to whom whatever Lenin had said half a century ago was of no concern, saw the Communists as the epitome of national betrayal. In a country that had only recently gained national independence such an accusation leveled against a political organization is tantamount to the death sentence.

Were the Chinese leaders aware of this? Of course they were. Could they have foreseen such a reaction? Undoubtedly.

The concept of the Indian Communist party as an alternative to the then ruling Congress party and as an organization that could unite all the country's left-wing forces was smashed with one blow. The possibility of the Indian Communists coming to power on a nationwide scale lost all reality, not only for the immediate future but also for the foreseeable future.

The blow, aimed carefully and cruelly, was right on the mark.

It was now Indonesia's turn.

Some time in the future, when all the circumstances hinging on the events that resulted in the massacre of the Indonesian Communists become known, the complete story of China's role in the events may be told. But even today the fact that Suharto seemed to be so well informed about the imminent coup is more than just strange. Prepared and inspired by Peking, the attempted coup failed and, moreover, resulted in the banning of the Indonesian Communist party and the execution of its entire leadership together with hundreds of thousands of rank and file party members. It is fairly obvious that this outcome certainly suited Mao Tse-tung much more than a Communist victory in Indonesia for that would certainly have led to the appearance in the leadership of the revolutionary movement of a rival powerful enough to show the Asians an alternative, non-Chinese road to Socialism.

The Chinese leaders regard the drive for unity and territorial integrity as a prerequisite for the success of any undertaking. Since success or, in the Chinese phraseology, victory must be achieved at any price, it stands to reason that no price can be too high in attaining the prerequisite of victory, that is, integrity and unity. If that purpose can be achieved only by sacrificing the Communist parties of other countries, they must be sacrificed. If it can be achieved only by killing hundreds of thousands of Chinese, they must be killed.

And hundreds of thousands of Chinese were killed in Manchuria to ensure the unity of China and prevent secession. The offensive mounted in this area by the Joint Northeastern Anti-Japanese Army, the Fourth Army, and other military units belonging to both the Kuomintang and the Communists was spearheaded more against the forces of the Manchurian government than against the Japanese. This follows quite plainly from the facts adduced by Sun Tse concerning the action of the Fourth Army in Manchuria. In terms of numbers the ratio of Japanese troops and Manchurian government forces taking part in the fighting was 1 : 5. This means that only one out of every six bullets fired by the Communist Chinese soldiers could be expected to hit a Japanese soldier while the other five were calculated to hit Manchu soldiers. Another interesting point is the national makeup of these only one-sixth anti-Japanese and five-sixths anti-Manchurian forces. "As regards the origins of the officers and men of the Fourth Army," Sun Tse wrote, "almost all the localities and nationalities of China were represented. Not only Chinese, but also Koreans, and representatives of some Mongol peoples, and Moslems." The surprising point is that there were no Manchu in the rank of the Fourth Army operating in Manchuria. However small a percentage of China's total population, they certainly outnumbered the Moslems, Mongol, or Koreans who were singled out for special mention by Sun Tse. The simple explanation is that the Manchu proper were all fighting on the other side—among those who were trying to uphold the independence of the country in which they once used to constitute the majority.

The much-vaunted anti-Japanese struggle in Manchuria was therefore in effect an anti-Manchurian struggle, a full-scale colonial war. It was a war in which anything that stood for the independence of the country and for its secession from China was ruthlessly killed.

It was by no means fortuitous that Manchuria became an arena of the final phases in the struggle between the Kuomintang and the Communists for hegemony in Mainland China. At the end of 1946 after the defeat of Japan, the Kuomintang caught the Communists completely unawares by landing a huge force in southern Manchuria. Despite the presence of Soviet forces which had handed over to the

Communists all the armaments captured from the Japanese Kwantung Army, it took them a full three years to "pacify" the territory.

Even so, the roots of Manchurian independence were far too strong to be destroyed through punitive military action alone. To neutralize the urge for independence required a lengthy period of complex political and administrative maneuvering. A territory where the tradition of independence was still very much alive and which had enjoyed at least a measure of formal independence for so long could not be turned into a Chinese province even by force of arms. This is why Peking initially had to agree to the continued functioning of an autonomous government in Manchuria. Later, in 1952–1954, it was gradually abolished and the autonomy ended. Simultaneously, those who under the obtaining conditions seemed to personify the concept of Manchuria's independence, namely Kao Kang, who then headed the autonomous Communist government of Manchuria, were also removed from power. The list of accusations against Kao Kang included the charge that in 1949 he had visited Moscow at the head of a Manchurian trade and industrial mission and that, while in Russia, he had negotiated agreements on behalf of Manchuria as some kind of independent administrative and political entity. In fact, however, Kao Kang had been acting in complete accord with the traditional status of Manchuria whose independence had been recognized by Moscow in 1941. Accused of attempting to recreate Manchuria's independence, Kao Kang promptly vanished from the political scene. But that was probably not enough for the Chinese and in 1955 Kao Kang was officially reported to have committed suicide. With his death there was no other political leader left to epitomize the idea of an independent Manchuria.

And so, gradually, step by step, Peking achieved its aim and Manchuria was deprived of its independence, its autonomy, the last vestiges of its identity, and even of its own name. In the very early phases of the drive to return Manchuria to China, particularly during the military "pacification" of the area, one man especially distinguished himself. His name was Lin Piao and until fairly recently he was Chairman Mao's heir apparent. What he accomplished in Manchuria was much more than a victory over a country which wanted to achieve its independence. By cutting short Manchuria's bid for independence he discouraged others from attempting to break away and thus preserved the integrity of China. The man who did that certainly earned the right—albeit unconsummated—to be the great Mao's successor and to stand next to him atop the towering reviewing stand on Tienanmen Square in Peking.

The example of the Suppressor of Manchuria, Lin Piao, is deeply symbolic. While Lin's political career—and indeed his very life—ended in utter disgrace, the three-million-strong Manchurian people are still very much alive. But though far less numerous peoples elsewhere enjoy autonomy, independence, and even United Nations membership, the people of Manchuria have been robbed of all these cherished attributes of nationhood. But for how long?

# 2

# THE MONGOLS: A STUDY IN DICHOTOMY

## *Beyond the Chinese Border*

In January 1978 a session of the People's Congress of Inner Mongolia was held. Addressing the session, Yu Tai-chun, Chinese and Chairman of the Revolutionary Committee of this autonomous district, said, using the traditional phraseology: "[R]elentlessly following the Central Committee of our Party headed by its wise leader, Chairman Hua Ko-feng, we shall exert every effort to turn this autonomous region into a steel bulwark of the Party along the northern border of our country against imperialism and revisionism."

The most interesting thing is not what was said and, perhaps, not even the fact that a Chinese spoke on behalf of the Mongolians. Most interesting is that the Mongolians proper accounted for only 33 percent of the total number of delegates to the session. In other words, the Mongolians had become a minority in their own country. But this is only the first part of the problem.

The second part is far more dramatic. According to the latest statistics, there are 14 Chinese settlers to every Mongolian in Inner Mongolia. So the ratio between Mongolians and Chinese at the People's Congress should also be 1 : 14 but the ratio is quite clearly 1 : 3.

What has induced the Chinese authorities to allow the Mongolians, if not the majority of votes, at least such a great advantage in contrast to the actual demographic ratio? It is well known that regarding the national minorities Peking will never waive its position of leadership. What then made it do so in 1978?

To answer this question it seems most logical to take a view of Inner Mongolia from the other side of the border.

The Ulan-Bator of today does not look as exotic as one would expect. It is a growing, modern city, with wide streets, comfortable housing, multistorey hotels. There is opera and ballet and a circus and it is safe to drink the tap water. In the spacious new restaurant I was pleased to see our neighbors at the next table, a group of Japanese businessmen, being served East German beer. I asked for a bottle too, but was refused. When I complained to the manager I was told that East German beer was only for foreigners. Later on some of my Mongolian friends explained politely, "Well, you should take it as a compliment that we do not consider you a foreigner! Our Russian friends are very dear to us and as for the beer, it is simply kept for VIPs and delegations."

Although Russians are not thought of as foreigners in Mongolia and the countries have the closest of ties—almost all Mongolia's imported goods are of Soviet origin and her intellectuals received their education in the USSR—all the same it does not take long for the wife of a Mongolian official to realize that there are more exciting cities in the world than nearby Irkutsk and that Chanel No. 5 smells better than "Red Moscow." No wonder French perfume and brandy and Scotch have already found their way to Mongolia. The 60 Mercedes-Benz saloons purchased from West Germany were easy winners in a competition for comfort with the Soviet Volgas.

The country's geographical location between the two Communist giants has forced the Mongolians to be careful diplomats in their relations with China.

It is becoming quite the thing nowadays to compare Mongolia's capital, Ulan-Bator, with Hong Kong. The differences between the great, bustling port and the young city in the windswept upland valley are obvious but the similarity lies in the role of each as a listening post for the outside world to follow what is going on in China. Hong Kong, upon Chinese insistence, has instituted all manner of restrictions for

Russia and her allies and, partly as a result, Ulan-Bator has become a most important listening post for Chinese specialists from Communist countries. They can work here in a normal atmosphere and naturally what goes on in Peking is of prime interest to them.

The communication line from Ulan-Bator to Moscow is the only one in the world which runs so close to Peking and yet is still reliable, with no chance of Chinese interception.

Prime Minister Tsedenbal was optimistic about Peking when I spoke to him on my visit to Ulan-Bator, saying, "I hope the negotiations will reach a successful conclusion." Talking about his own country, he said, "Our government tried and is still trying to restore our former good relationship with China, but unfortunately we do not meet with any reciprocity from the Chinese side."

From Ulan-Bator I traveled by rail all the way to the Chinese border. One of the passenger coaches in the train goes straight through to Peking. (About 6000 Chinese live in Ulan-Bator where they have their own club with their usual propaganda material displayed outside.) The few Chinese making the long journey never had a chance to walk along the corridor to the restaurant car. The connecting door remained firmly locked and the only sign of life was the portrait of Mao smiling through the glass. The Chinese passengers would wave their red books to passersby at each station and at the border station an engine steamed in from the Chinese side. It was decorated with slogans in both Chinese and Mongolian and bore an enormous sooty portrait of the Chairman on the front.

The stretch of railway line which runs for 1114 kilometers (668 miles) through Mongolia from the Soviet border to that with China was until recently among the busiest in the world. Now it carries only 15 percent of the former passenger traffic and only 4 percent of the freight.

During recent years the Mongolians have amassed a sad record of facts, lists of cargo addressed to Vietnam and delayed on ridiculous pretexts. The Chinese have reconstructed the track running from their side of the border, changing it from wide to narrow gauge. The Mongolians also complain that they have been put to enormous expense recently because goods in transit to North Korea or Japan are no longer permitted by the Chinese to be shipped the short way across Chinese territory and via Chinese ports. Instead they have to be sent about twice the distance and shipped from a Russian port.

Trade with China itself has come almost to a standstill.

When I asked Prime Minister Tsedenbal whether he agreed that Mongolia was yet another divided country, like Korea or Vietnam, he answered negatively. His argument was that one cannot draw such a comparison because Inner Mongolia is within the boundaries of another Socialist country.

Today that argument must obviously be reassessed. Several of the latest official handbooks to appear in Moscow make it quite clear that the Soviet Union no longer lists China among the countries belonging to the "Socialist Camp." Mongolia's leaders, who usually toe the Soviet line, will no doubt also correct their attitude.


## A Nation Divided

The Mongol nation gave the world Genghis Khan.

It was from the steppes of Mongolia that the hordes of mounted warriors overran China, Asia, and half of Europe. For everyone else the history of the Mongol invasion is a story written in blood. For the Mongols the memory of Genghis Khan and his campaigns is a source of inexhaustible pride and national glory. To this day Mongolian eyes begin to sparkle as their owner recalls the time when, in the words of a modern Mongolian author, there existed "a vast Mongol Empire, which in the 13th and 14th centuries laid claim to world domination and held a multitude of countries in subjection."

The weight of Mongolia in world affairs today is but a shadow of its erstwhile might and power. But even so it is a shadow that covers a lot of land. Just one part of Mongolia proper, the Mongolian People's Republic, occupies an area exceeding Britain, France, Portugal, and Ireland taken together. After Soviet Russia and China, the Mongolian People's Republic is the biggest Socialist country. And it is the only Communist country in Asia which unequivocally toes the Soviet line through thick and thin.

Historically Mongolia, like Manchuria, was outside the boundaries of China. Situated beyond the Great Wall, the country was regarded by the Chinese themselves as a foreign land. When members of a Russian mission on their way to Peking once asked some Chinese officials, "What is that wall for which runs from the sea to the Bukhars?" (meaning Eastern Turkestan), they were told that "the wall runs from the sea to the Bukhars because there are two lands, one Mugal (that is, Mongolian), the other Chinese, and that is the boundary between them."

In the seventeenth century Mongolia was conquered and incorporated into the Chinese Empire. That part of it which is today known as the Mongolian People's Republic regained its independence in 1911. Its traditional name is Outer Mongolia as distinct from Inner Mongolia, which is still within the political frontiers of China. The geographical boundary between the two Mongolias is the Gobi Desert. But it was political not geographical reasons that underlay the existence of two Mongolias. Initially, the division into Inner and Outer Mongolia merely reflected the different dates of the Manchu conquest.[1]

The age-old terminological distinction acquired a new meaning several decades ago when Outer Mongolia broke away from China to form a separate state, the Mongolian People's Republic. In the process a numerically greater part of the Mongols remained inside the state boundaries of China. For them the struggle for national liberation is far from over.

As in other areas which fell under Chinese colonial domination, the struggle has been going on for as many years as the domination itself. I have no intention of boring the reader with a detailed account of the ups and downs of the struggle. Uprisings followed one upon the other, punctuated only by severe reprisals which took a dire toll of the people in the recalcitrant provinces. Suffice it to say that in putting down just one uprising in 1892 the Chinese troops killed around 30,000 Mongols.

Hardly had the grass covered the graves of the dead when a new uprising broke out at Urga in 1905. It was followed by severe fighting between the Mongols and Chinese forces at Tsitsihar in 1909–1910.

---

[1] In contrast to China, which the Manchu brought to heel fairly rapidly, it took them over one hundred years (from 1636 to 1755) to conquer Mongolia.

Each one of these uprisings had its own dramatic history, its own heroes and victims. But news of the events rarely filtered through to Europe. And even if many months or even years later some European newspaper did print a report on the subject, events taking place somewhere in a remote corner of the Chinese Empire left everyone completely indifferent.

At the time each generation of Mongols regarded the diplomatic stratagems of their chieftains and the military ploys of their famous war leaders and insurgents as being in the very focus of world events. Today it is locked away between the pages of long-forgotten books or in the minds of the few scholars who have dedicated themselves to studying the history of Mongolia.

Without attempting to record the history of the anticolonial struggle of the Mongols, let me emphasize just one of its salient features. It is a highly symptomatic feature—and one that helps one to gain an insight not so much into the past as into the present and—possibly—the future of that nation.

In its struggle against Chinese colonization, Eastern Turkestan has always turned toward Central Asia for help. Tibet has always looked to the Buddhist world. But the eyes of the Mongols have always been turned toward Russia. It would, of course, be more than naïve to explain this by any feelings of love for the Russians on the part of the Mongols. In fact, the relationship is something that has its own roots in history, something that has become a kind of national tradition. Among the underlying factors is the existence inside Russia of lands populated both by Mongols proper and by peoples who are their close kinsmen and blood brothers. These are the Buryats of Siberia and the Kalmycks of the Volga valley. Linked with them through bonds of religious, historical, linguistic, and cultural affinity, the Mongols treated their kinsmen residing beyond the boundaries of the Chinese Empire as a source of spiritual and sometimes material support in their struggle for independence. So it was a natural urge for routed Mongol insurgents and their defeated leaders to seek refuge in Russian territory. The fact that this tradition was an enduring one is amply evidenced by some of the letters addressed by the Mongols to the Russian authorities. One such letter reads, "We request advice and assistance in securing an untroubled life in view of the following. . . ." What followed was a detailed description of the religious

and territorial oppression practiced by the Chinese colonial administration. "It is their desire," the letter ends, "to destroy down to the
last root not only us, Mongol resettlers, but also all Mongols of the
Western and Southern provinces together with our yellow faith. Such
is the grievous woe that we do foresee. And whatever happens, we
must have arms and increase our forces."

While refraining from any overt interference in events across the
border, the Russian frontier authorities nonetheless often found ways
to help the Mongols. Sometimes the assistance assumed the form of
monetary support. Thus, Prince Udai of Jasaktu received from the
Russian government the considerable sum of 20,000 rubles. On other
occasions, the Mongols entreated the Russian government to grant
them citizenship rights or else they simply crossed the border into
Russia together with their herds.

## The Thorny Road to Unity

With the fall of the imperial regime in China the issue of Mongolia's
independence almost automatically came to the fore as a practical
proposition.

On December 1, 1911, Outer Mongolia was declared a republic.
Two weeks later the Bogdo-Gegen, Djuabutsun-Damba, mounted the
throne at Urga, or Ulan-Bator as it is known today. Adopting the title
Elevated By Many, he became the spiritual and temporal ruler of the
new state which was thus reborn after two centuries of foreign rule.

Since then there have always been two Mongolias. Inner Mongolia
was a bit too slow in the uptake but it too made a rather belated
attempt to secede from China in a peaceful and orderly manner by
invoking an imperial decree dating back to the period of Mongolia's
conquest. According to the decree, should there be a change of dynasty in China the Mongols were free to revert to their previous state
and live in accordance with their own original laws. The princes of
Inner Mongolia made no bones about informing the new republican
government of China of their intention to exercise their right to
disassociate themselves from China. The Chinese responded by send-

ing in troops. But Inner Mongolia had no intention of surrendering. In 1916 twenty-four Mongol princes assembled in Peking to present a memorandum to Yuan Shi-kai confirming that, unless the Manchu dynasty was restored, the Mongol princes and rulers would secede from China. Since that time secession from China and unification with Outer Mongolia have been synonymous for Inner Mongolia. But it was plain even then that since the one real opportunity had been missed, the goal could be achieved only through force of arms, not through memorandums, negotiations, or references to historical documents. Though Mao's famous phrase about power being born out of the barrel of a gun was to be uttered only a few decades later, the reality that gave rise to it had always existed in China. Added proof of its validity—if any were needed—was provided by the fate of Prince Udai of Inner Mongolia.

Udai made no attempt to raise an insurrection or to begin hostilities against the Chinese. Very properly, and in compliance with all the requirements of international law, he announced that his principality was uniting with Outer Mongolia and requested the Chinese colonial administration to leave his land. The reaction to this took the form of a punitive expedition of Chinese troops which went on a rampage throughout the territory of the principality.

Many years later the world was to shudder with horror when it learned of the tragedy of Lidice, the village in Czechoslovakia, which the Nazis razed to the ground, having first killed all the inhabitants. In Inner Mongolia there were dozens of Lidices but no one in the world ever found out. Patiently and diligently, as if it were just another job to be done, the Chinese soldiers would put to death in cold blood entire villages—sparing neither young nor old, man nor beast.

As far back as 1911, anticipating a long and bloody struggle, the princes of Inner Mongolia had petitioned Czar Nicholas II for assistance and arms to fight the Chinese. Arms were sent and assistance was promised. No less intensively the princes set about purchasing arms in Japan. As subsequent events were to prove, the purchase of arms was a far-sighted act for in the years to come the struggle for the reunification of Mongolia was in fact waged on two fronts—military as well as diplomatic.

On the military side the Mongols mustered a fairly powerful force.

The strength of their units armed with cannons and machine guns sometimes numbered several thousand. They inflicted considerable defeats on regular Chinese forces and at times they had entire provinces under their control. But isolated successes in the anti-colonial war could not determine its final outcome. Inner Mongolia began to seek help and support from its brothers in Outer Mongolia.

In 1912 a special mission arrived at Urga from Inner Mongolia to ask the Bogdo-Gegen for aid in fighting the Chinese forces. In 1913 and 1914, seeing that the Bogdo-Gegen was powerless to provide such aid, Inner Mongolia made several appeals to the Russian government. The Mongols begged the czar to protect their rights, property, and "yellow faith" from China. This urge to escape from Chinese domination and to unify the people within the framework of one state continued in 1914 and 1915. Inner Mongolia's pleas for unity were joined by those of the Urga government as well. Thus, Mongolia's prime minister, Sain Noyan-Khan, in a letter to Russia's foreign minister, Sazonov, particularly insisted "on such a definition of the boundaries of the Mongol State as would incorporate within it all Mongols desirous of joining."

The fact that neither the diplomatic nor the military efforts of the Mongols to bring about their unification had any success is easily explained. The Russian government had to pursue a very cautious policy in the area. While supporting Inner Mongolia's demands for reunification, St. Petersburg had to couch such support in a form that would not affect the interests of Japan, which regarded Inner Mongolia as a part of its own sphere of influence. The Russian government could not risk damaging relations with Japan while the wounds inflicted by the recent Russo-Japanese War were still fresh. The most important reason, however, was that Russia could on no account face a possible conflict in the East at a time when her entire strength was taken up by the war on her extended western flank—from the Baltic to the Black Sea.

Yet these reasons, however valid and convincing, in a sense touched only the surface of the problem. Underneath lay its very heart. It is still a problem for which no answer has been found to this day: On what basis was the reunification of Mongolia to come about?

If Inner Mongolia had simply joined Outer Mongolia, then, as now, under Russian influence, the net result would have been a vast increase in Russia's influence in the area. This neither Japan nor China could ever accept.

If Outer Mongolia had joined Inner Mongolia, which in the 20s and 30s was under Japanese influence and later reverted to Chinese control, the result would have been a similar expansion of the sphere of Japanese or Chinese influence at great cost to Soviet positions. This Moscow could never accept.

So the reunification of the Mongols within a single state thus proved to be an issue extending far beyond the interests of the Mongols alone. It became a bone of contention in relations among such political giants as the Soviet Union, Japan, and China—not to mention the United States which could not remain indifferent to any shift in the balance of forces in this part of Asia.

The problem of Mongolia as a nation split in two defies any simple solution. In this sense it bears a striking resemblance to the case of present-day East and West Germany. Though both Communist and Western leaders know and admit that the situation in Central Europe is an abnormal one, they are powerless to formulate any simple solutions which could lead to a restoration of the German people's unity. Unification based on the East German Communist pattern would result in extending Communist influence on Central Europe. To this the Western democracies could never agree. At the same time, extension of the political system operating in the Federal Republic of Germany to the territory of the German Democratic Republic would entail a loss for the Communists which they too could never countenance.

The problem of nations divided in two by diametrically opposite political systems is one that affects great political communities and involves much more than the destinies of the nations directly concerned. Korea is an example—a nation which, like Mongolia and Germany, is also cut in half by a frontier line.

Although today such situations are no longer regarded as isolated political freaks and we can now attempt to treat them as an enduring fact of modern political life, this was most decidedly not the case in the 20s when Mongolia became the first nation to be split up between the Capitalist and the Communist worlds.

## The Long Road to Unity

Seeking to avoid any complications on its Far Eastern flank, the Soviet Union did its best, at least formally, to dissociate itself from the idea of the reunification of Outer and Inner Mongolia, leaving it entirely in the hands of the Mongols themselves. What is more, anticipating the likelihood of excesses, the Soviets went out of their way to emphasize that they did not support the idea of reunification in general. This was stated in no uncertain terms on the pages of the magazine *Revolutsionny Vostok (Revolutionary East)*. "Can Outer Mongolia meet the demands of the economic and cultural development of the two Mongolias if it is incapable of solving its own problems?" the magazine queried. "The reply to this question is plain to anyone who is possessed of common sense." These words, which were certainly noted in the West, were addressed primarily to Ulan-Bator. The leadership of the Mongolian People's Republic, in the person of Choibalsan and his associates, was fully determined to bring about the reunification of both Mongolias—by armed force if necessary. It was probably because all chances of bringing pressure to bear upon the Mongolian leaders through the traditional party channels were exhausted that Moscow had to resort to such a step as the publication of the article in *Revolutsionny Vostok*. Moscow was thereby publicly and deliberately refusing to share responsibility with the Mongolian leaders for any action they might take.

This demarche may well have been the final step discouraging Choibalsan from trying to reunify Mongolia by force. Until then such an attempt had seemed very likely. This was evidenced not only by Moscow's reaction but also by the preparations that had been under way in Inner Mongolia. In 1925 there had already been a First Congress of the People's Revolutionary Party of Inner Mongolia. In the same year a center for the formation of a People's Revolutionary Army of Inner Mongolia had been set up at Kalgan. According to the rather fragmentary reports that filtered through to the West, some of its units actually conducted hostilities against the Chinese forces and even made several attempts to capture a few towns. But their main objective was obviously to render support to the forces of Outer Mongolia, when and if they ultimately decided to enter the territory of Inner Mongolia.

However, as we have seen, the plan for Mongolia's unification by force was not supported by Moscow and was never carried out. It is easy to understand the feelings of bitterness and disappointment that must have engulfed Ulan-Bator at this letdown by the Russian allies. The sin was doubly exculpated at a later date, when Stalin no less vigorously resisted another plan calling for the military unification of Mongolia—a plan which this time emanated not from Ulan-Bator but from Tokyo.

Since the establishment of Manchukuo, Japan had planned and persistently carried out her intention of using the new state as a bridgehead for penetrating deep into Asia. One of the first steps in this far-reaching policy was the setting up on the territory of Manchukuo of an Autonomous Mongolian Government. Established on the basis of Mongol-inhabited areas, this government, regardless of whatever actual authority it exercised, if any, did provide a center of political gravity. Prior to its existence there had only been one magnetic pole of Mongolian statehood—Ulan-Bator; now it was opposed by another. All those forces which were striving for the establishment of an independent Inner Mongolia yet were loath to follow in the footsteps of the Mongolian People's Republic now had the option of adhering to the opposite political pole. This tactic was not slow in bearing fruit. Several of the Mongol principalities of Inner Mongolia declared their desire to join Manchukuo and swore allegiance to the Autonomous Mongolian Government.

At the same time, with Japan's supervision and encouragement, political forces began to mature in Inner Mongolia itself and were soon ready for action. Domtsuklor, or Prince Teh, set up an Autonomous Military Government of Inner Mongolia. This government, which was under Japan's aegis, was nonetheless recognized in 1937 by Nanking. The hopes for autonomy or even independence with which some inhabitants of Inner Mongolia linked the formation of this puppet government turned out to be illusory—as could easily have been predicted. Inner Mongolia and its political leaders were assigned the role of pawns in the game of power politics. Referring to the

Mongols under Japanese or Chinese control, Owen Lattimore has written that "they were given orders, and if they did not obey, they were imprisoned or shot."

Owen Lattimore made several other significant observations. In the 30s some of the political leaders of Inner Mongolia confidentially told him about their plan for a military reunification of Mongolia. Inner Mongolian forces, armed and trained by Japan, were to invade the Mongolian People's Republic, overthrow the existing government with the support of the local priests and establish a single state uniting all Mongols. It was particularly emphasized that Japanese troops would not take part in such action as their presence might provoke a wave of patriotism in Outer Mongolia and thus mobilize the people to resist the invasion.

It is easy to see that in effect this was a copy of Choibalsan's plan only turned inside out. And it contained the same basic flaw in failing to take into account the fact that powerful political forces situated beyond its boundaries were very much interested in the fate of Mongolia. This became particularly clear in 1936 when Stalin made a sensational statement in an interview with Roy Howard. He said that should the Mongolian People's Republic be attacked, the Soviet Union would render it all-out assistance.

The warning was a timely one. Evidently Stalin had learned of some of Japan's secret plans in respect to Mongolia. He may have been familiar with Prime Minister Tanaka's secret memorandum which pointed out that "to conquer China we must first conquer Manchuria and Mongolia." Or perhaps he may have known about the no less authoritative statement by General Araki, the Japanese war minister: "Japan does not want to allow the existence of such an equivocal territory as is Mongolia, bordering directly on Japan's sphere of influence, Manchuria and China. Mongolia will in any event have to belong to us territorially."

Three years after Stalin made his statement the firmness of the Soviet Union's position toward Mongolia was confirmed in the fighting at Khalkin-gol. Realizing, after Stalin's statement, that in any invasion of Outer Mongolia it would be up against Soviet, not Mongolian, regular forces, Tokyo made a change of plans and decided to employ as a strike force the Japanese army, not the troops of Inner

Mongolia. According to Soviet figures, 60,000 Japanese officers and men were killed or wounded in the fighting which ended with the rout of the Japanese invading force. But even the Japanese casualty figures (17,000) provide a striking picture of the scale of their defeat—a defeat both military and political.

In the ensuing years new events in the form of World War II temporarily removed the question of Mongolia's reunification from the agenda. The world powers had too many other things on their minds. But not the Mongols, who could not remain oblivious for a single instant to the dismemberment of their nation and were but waiting for a convenient occasion to return to what was for them a burning issue. Their chance seemed to come with the start of the Soviet army's campaign against Japan. Could there indeed be a better opportunity for carrying out the long-awaited Choibalsan plan to reunify Mongolia by force?

When 80,000 soldiers of the Mongolian People's Republic supported by the Red Army invaded Inner Mongolia and overran it within a matter of days many people thought the unification of Mongolia had at last become a fact. In light of this, two things are worthy of special mention. Firstly, the strength of Mongolia's own contingent. It is certainly quite obvious that for a nation of 750,000 people to muster an army of 80,000 meant making a very big effort. And secondly, it is quite plain that the effort was not prompted by military need. Clearly, had there been not 80,000 but 40,000 or even 30,000 Mongol troops, the outcome of the war in the Far East would have been the same. The severe strain to which that little country put itself was therefore provoked by something more than purely military consideration, namely political motives. The task of the Mongolian forces was to take control over Inner Mongolia rather than simply to inflict a military defeat on the Japanese army.

Highly indicative in this respect was the statement put out by the Mongolian government and the Small Hural on August 10, 1945. Declaring a "holy war" on Japan, the statement pointed out that the Mongolian army was entering the war for the sake of "once and forever ending the oppression and humiliation suffered by the Mongol tribes at the hands of foreign invaders." In other words, for the sake of liberating Inner Mongolia.

The belief that Ulan-Bator was entering into the war in the hope of achieving a final settlement to the Mongolian problem (that is, re-unification of Mongolia) is borne out by the active propaganda drive undertaken by the Mongolian army units as soon as they pressed into Inner Mongolia. As the Moscow periodical *Novoye Vremya (New Times)* wrote at the time, "The troops' tour of the villages in the newly liberated country inhabited by their kinsmen was a striking illustration of what twenty-five years of independence have given the Mongolian people."

Apart from the propaganda efforts made by the Mongol soldiers, their very presence on Mongolian soil as liberators was the most convincing argument in favor of reunification. Splendidly uniformed and well trained, courteous in their treatment of the population, and fully confident in the righteousness of their Communist ideology, they provided a striking contrast to the other soldiers who had trampled the soil of long-suffering Inner Mongolia—notably the Japanese and Chinese troops. This time they were soldiers who spoke the same language as the local population for they were their *own* soldiers. For the first time public opinion in Inner Mongolia was not divided regarding the future of the country. In Ulan-Bator Marshal Choibal-san was deluged by an endless stream of letters, resolutions, and appeals from Inner Mongolia, all requesting permission for Inner Mongolia to join the Mongolian People's Republic.

These sentiments took hold of the masses—and not only in Inner Mongolia. On October 20, 1945, an "unofficial" referendum on the reunification of the two parts of the country was held in Outer Mongolia as well. Though the position of the Mongols on this question was quite plain even without any referendum, Choibalsan obviously staged it to obtain one more argument in his favor—in the form of public opinion.

The destiny of Inner Mongolia appeared to be a foregone conclusion, while the wisdom of Stalin, who had suspended the Choibalsan plan when it was premature but had now permitted it to take its course, was obvious. But Stalin once again displayed his wisdom to the Mongols, this time to their very great displeasure.

It is probably too much to hope that the negotiations that went on at that time between Moscow and China will ever be made known to the public. But as far as may be judged, China's position in respect to Mongolia was so intractable that Moscow had to give way. In the past Moscow had had to back down from Mongolia's reunification in the face of a Japanese threat. Now Moscow again had to back down, this time under pressure from China.

When I say that the negotiations will probably never become public property, I mean not only their content, but also the question of which of the two Chinas was negotiating with the Kremlin: Mao's China or Chiang Kai-shek's. But in this particular question there is hardly any difference.

It will be recalled that almost until its last hour the Kuomintang stubbornly refused to recognize the independent existence of even the Mongolian People's Republic, not to mention the granting of independence to Inner Mongolia. It is a characteristic fact that when the Soviet–Mongolian protocol of 1924 was published, the Chinese Foreign Ministry sent the Soviet government a protest note saying, "In so far as Outer Mongolia is an integral part of the Chinese Republic, no foreign state may conclude with it any treaties or agreements."

This implacable position which asserted the inalienability from China of both Outer and, still more, Inner Mongolia was reaffirmed in numerous subsequent documents. In 1930 the Nanking government convened a special conference for this purpose which reiterated that "Mongolia and Tibet are integral parts of the Chinese Republic and the peoples of Mongolia and Tibet are Chinese citizens, and the Chinese government will have to protect them from foreign aggressive policies."

Ulan-Bator's policies in Inner Mongolia were reversed. Mongolian troops began to be withdrawn. The "provisional government of the Republic of Inner Mongolia," which had set its sights on unification and secession from China, was disbanded. The man who did so was Ulanfu, a graduate of Sun Yat-sen University in Moscow and a trusted follower of Mao. It is interesting to note that it was he who led the new government of the Autonomous Region of Inner Mongolia which was set up in 1947.

As soon as the last Mongol soldiers had left Inner Mongolia the frontier posts and signs were reinstalled along the entire length of the boundary, those same posts and signs which the Mongolian tankmen had uprooted with such fervor when they crossed the border and pressed southwards through the Gobi Desert. And once again, as many times before, it was shown that the problem of Mongolia's unification could be resolved anywhere—in Tokyo, Peking, or Moscow—but not in Ulan-Bator or Huhehot, capital of Inner Mongolia. Though this prospect offers the Mongols no cause for rejoicing, there is still nothing humiliating about it. On the contrary, it attests to the importance attached to the Mongolian issue. It is said that all things have their price. This surely includes the historical importance of a nation's destiny. The greater the importance, the higher the price. Some pay the price in blood, like Russia, others in the Diaspora, like the Jews or Armenians. And some are destined to share the fate of Mongolia.

## The Struggle Continues

It is hard to imagine any nation ever reconciling itself to such a fate. Restoration of the Sino-Mongolian frontier, which still cuts through the very heart of Mongolia, could least of all provide a lasting solution. This was but a postponement of the solution.

Once installed in Inner Mongolia, the Chinese administration promptly took action to block all avenues for the leakage of undesirable information about events in the area. And yet there is enough evidence today to believe that in recent years, far from abating, the drive for reunification with Outer Mongolia has in fact become even stronger. Proof of this has been found in reports relating to events linked with, or directly caused by, the Cultural Revolution.

A number of news items coming out of China have dealt with manifestations of so-called "local nationalism" in Inner Mongolia. This term is currently being used by the colonial authorities in Peking to denote the desire of the Mongols for national independence and for reunification as a nation state.

The wave of resurgent nationalism in Inner Mongolia was confirmed in recent years by the building of the tomb of Genghis Khan. The interesting point here is that although it obviously ran counter to Peking's policy in the area, the Chinese administration proved powerless to prevent the construction. It has been asserted in Peking that the favorite slogan of the Mongols is "Mongolia for the Mongols! Sons of Genghis Khan, unite!"

Among the large-character posters prominently displayed in Peking at this time was one accusing Ulanfu of having initiated the slogan "Mongolia for the Mongols!" Ulanfu, who was ousted during the Cultural Revolution, was also accused of "subverting the unity of China" and wanting to unite Inner and Outer Mongolia.

Whether and in what measure Ulanfu in person was indeed the guilty party is beside the point. Such identification of "all evils" with one individual is a traditional propaganda ploy. In this case it is not the target of Peking's propaganda attacks that is important but the attacks themselves—or rather the specific charges behind them. These were quite plainly directly concerned with separatism and specifically related to the ever-present demands for secession from China and reunification with the Mongolian People's Republic. Moreover, it has been reported that some Mongolians are prepared to divide Inner Mongolia into "purely Mongol" areas and into areas with a predominantly Chinese population so as to be able to demand the separation from China of at least the Mongolian areas. They are apparently even willing to sacrifice to China the steel mill at Paotow and the railroad as a price for their independence.

The separatist movement must surely have acquired considerable proportions if the Revolutionary Committee of the Autonomous Region of Inner Mongolia had to coin a special name, "nation splitter," for its followers. According to the science of logic a term designating a phenomenon is usually introduced only after that phenomenon has overstepped a certain threshold of repetition. It has indeed been admitted by the Chinese Communist press, averse as it usually is to any such admissions, that the number of "nation splitters" in Inner Mongolia is sufficiently great. "The enemies are everywhere," *Neimengu jih pao* (the *Inner Mongolia Daily*) stated in an editorial, "in political organs, in the sphere of economics, culture, and education; they are operating as an 'independent underground kingdom.' "

It is interesting to note that the identification of "all evils" with the person of Ulanfu has had an effect that could hardly have been anticipated by Chinese propaganda. All that constituted a crime in Peking's eyes can hardly have been regarded as such by the Mongols.

Moreover, the charges of Mongolian nationalism and the attempts to bring about secession from China promptly elevated Ulanfu to the status of a national hero. The Chinese governors of Inner Mongolia may have toppled Ulanfu from his position of power without much difficulty, but they have certainly been powerless to topple his prestige, built up in part by their own accusations. *Neimengu jih pao* wrote about "unceasing attacks by the followers of Ulanfu." It is common knowledge that a group of Mongols sent a delegation to Peking with instructions to fight for Ulanfu's rehabilitation. This was unprecedented in the history of the Cultural Revolution. In the words of the members of the delegation "the ouster of Ulanfu has led to the oppression of the Mongols." "If it is all over with Ulanfu," they declared, "then it is all over with us Mongols too."

Such an outcome would certainly have suited the Chinese authorities perfectly. However, the statement in question was more in the nature of an exercise in rhetoric than anything else. Both the Mongols and the Mongolian problem were there to stay even after the disappearance of Ulanfu from the political scene. In fact, with Ulanfu's ouster the Mongolian problem became even more acute for Ulanfu had all along been playing the role of a buffer in his attempts to soften Peking's pressure by doing a political balancing act.

The Chinese military authorities that operated—and still do—in Inner Mongolia have doubtless kept a record of action by Inner Mongolia's liberation forces. And the time will come for those records to be made public. Not now, though, for today they still pose too much danger for Peking.

Today these events, as well as all others from which present-day Chinese leaders strive to dissociate themselves, are ascribed to the activities of the "gang of four." In August 1977 *Hunchi (Red Flag)* magazine published an article by the first secretary of the Inner Mongolian Party Committee under a traditional title, "The Radiating Ideas of Mao Tse-tung Illumine Inner Mongolia." Written in very high-flown style, this article touches lightly upon the delicate question of Chinese–Mongolian relations within the region. The author deems it necessary to mention the "gang of four" which was driving a wedge between the different nations and thus "undermining national unity."

The few reports abut Chinese reprisals in Inner Mongolia that reach the outside world come mainly from refugees who escape to the

Mongolian People's Republic. At Ulan-Bator I was able to meet some of them.

Mrs. Tseren (35) is a Mongol who recently escaped from Inner Mongolia, bringing one of her three children with her. She told me of fantastic atrocities and humiliations which she and other Mongols suffered from the Chinese. She described tortures that took place in her own village—of people who were blinded or made to stand on heated stoves and of women whose breasts were branded with a hot iron. She described the incredible instruments of torture which sound like vestiges of the Middle Ages, including wooden yokes and braces lined with sharp nails. The victims were those who were suspected of belonging to a separatist movement. They were subjected to crude methods of indoctrination, made to chant Mao's phrases, and told: "You can live without food, but not without Mao's ideas." Mrs. Tseren said that she hoped the situation in China would change and that "other Socialist countries will help our people to survive."

Another curious feature is the reported participation of some Chinese in insurgent action on the side of the Mongols. Facts of this kind bring into still greater relief the scale of the centrifugal force operating in the outlying areas of China. It would thus appear that no sooner does a Chinese find himself in the territory of Manchuria, Eastern Turkestan, or Inner Mongolia than he falls prey to these separatist tendencies. And then from being a victim of such tendencies he turns into their exponent. True, this process is by no means a rapid one. Nor is it on a scale sufficient to neutralize the opposite effect—the strengthening of the bonds linking the territory concerned with the metropolis—which is the result of the forced migration of Chinese to the minority-populated lands.

## *Losing Your Language Is Like Losing Your Nationality*

The resettlement policy of the Chinese government in Inner Mongolia is traditional. In general terms it constitutes a repetition of the methods applied in Manchuria and Eastern Turkestan.

The start of this immigration explosion dates back to 1878 when the wave of Chinese colonization placed the Mongols face to face with numerous Chinese immigrants.

But this traditional policy of populating the colonies probably never came up against such stiff opposition in any other area as it did in Mongolia. In 1904 the Mongols used force in an attempt to wreck the immigration office. D. Davydov has written that among the unfavorable conditions for the settlement of Chinese in Mongolia is the hostility of the Mongols "who are very reluctant to yield their lands to the Chinese."

Nonetheless, the stubbornly persistent immigration policy, designed to cover more than one generation, continued unabated. It continued despite the resentment, protests, and resistance of the local population. As the wave of immigrants rolled deeper into Mongolia it was followed by the immigration offices which were in fact nothing but organs of colonial administration. By 1911 an immigration office was installed in the very heart of Outer Mongolia, in Urga.

A new epoch in the colonization and assimilation of Mongolia, like the other minority areas of China, began when Mao came to power.

In 1955 the Chinese-populated provinces of Suiyuan and Jehol and part of Ningsia province were incorporated in Inner Mongolia under the pretext of uniting all Mongol-populated lands. The result was that with one stroke of the administrative pen the Mongols were turned into an insignificant minority within their own national territory.

All this proceeded parallel with an intensified influx of Chinese immigrants. As one observer noted at the time, "the Mongols who live within China in Inner Mongolia have been so overrun by waves of Chinese immigrants in past years that they form no more than a small minority group in their own country." A convenient political excuse for stepping up this influx was provided by the construction at Paotow of a giant metallurgical plant. The rising towns and industrial centers are inhabited mostly by Chinese settlers. This has been noted by the few Western observers who have managed to visit Inner Mongolia. Summing up his observations on this subject, Klaus Menert has written: "When I compare my own impressions of Inner Mongolia of 1936 and 1957, I come to the conclusion that this area has been practically 'sinified' right up to the border between China and Outer Mongolia."

By 1950 there were already two Chinese for every Mongol in Inner Mongolia. By 1957 the ratio was 8 : 1. And by 1972 it was 14 : 1. The ratio was continuing to increase but no new data have been published after 1972.

What a painful wrench all this must have been for the local population. At one time the clashes between the Chinese immigrants, who began settling more and more territories in the area, and the local people assumed such a massive scale that Ulanfu had to call a special conference to try to reconcile the two hostile groups. One proof of this continuing enmity is provided by the Chinese propaganda efforts to prove the opposite.

In Mongolia, as in other national regions, Chinese immigrants and assimilation go hand in hand. Assimilation primarily affects the fields of language and culture. Very characteristically, in accusing Ulanfu of nationalism, the Chinese specifically blamed him for insisting on the equality of the Mongol and Chinese languages. In other words, from the Chinese point of view, the functional roles assigned to each of the two languages are very different. Even in this so-called national region it is the Chinese language that must be the predominant one. Ulanfu is not the only high-ranking Mongol downgraded during the Cultural Revolution who was on the receiving end of such charges. The intention behind all the charges—proffered as they are after the event—can hardly be to throw stones at departing shadows. More likely the intention is to inject into the popular mind a lasting association between the concepts of "Mongol language" and "Mongol culture" and such negative categories as "revisionist" or "capitalist roaders."

In this way, on Peking's initiative, a clear-cut stereotype of an approved and disapproved action is formed. Coming under the heading of disapproved is, notably, a desire to preserve the Mongol language. For instance, a former secretary of the city party committee of Huhehot was "dragged through the streets by the masses" for having "frenziedly encouraged the development of revisionism and nation splitting" by "forcing the masses to learn the spoken and written Mongol language." By contrast, approved action is the obliteration of the Mongol language by the Chinese language and the all-out sinification of the Mongol language.

A resolution passed by a conference on language questions which took place at Huhehot asserted that "the close relations between the Mongol and Han nationalities determine the close relations between the Mongol and Han languages. Therefore the absorption and borrowing of terms from the Han language for the enrichment and development of the Mongol language has become an objective and inevitable trend."

Similarly, a disapproved action—and one leading toward the splitting of China—is the protection and development of the national Mongol culture. This was in fact one of the charges against Ulanfu. And on the contrary, a strong desire to adopt Chinese culture, notably in its outward manifestations, is declared to be a publicly approved action for the Mongols. One Chinese mayor of a town in Inner Mongolia has said with reference to the Mongols: "Many of these speak Chinese, wear Chinese clothing, and to all intents and purposes have been assimilated by the Chinese."

Refugees from Inner Mongolia will tell you that the one and only official language in their country today is Chinese. It is used exclusively in all clerical work in all the official agencies and government. All tuition in secondary schools as well as in higher educational establishments is also in Chinese. Not a single book in the Mongol language is printed in Huhehot and the rare Mongol-language book which may still be found on the deserted shelves of the few bookshops in the town will be a translation from the Chinese.

The goal of this policy of suppressing and assimilating their national culture is, in the words of G.M. Frites, "to prevent the Inner Mongols from following the example of the independent Outer Mongols."

The process of the sinification of Inner Mongolia has gone a long way. Commenting on its results, Klaus Menert has written: "So, the only places left for a promising process of separatism are, in theory at least, Tibet and Sinkiang."

This assessment would have us believe that the Chinese have succeeded in dealing the death blow to Inner Mongolia as a national community. But the entire course of the Cultural Revolution and the reprisals it brought with it attest to the very opposite. They offer evidence of the indestructible desire of the Mongols to secede from China and unite within the framework of a single state. We would therefore be well advised to anticipate a continuing and lasting confrontation between Peking and Huhehot. In it Peking may well be expected to resort in the coming years to a method it has already applied in respect to Manchuria. Today, there is no longer any Manchuria on the map of China. Why should Inner Mongolia not disappear from the map in like manner? All the more so since there are but half as many Mongols in China as Manchu. Nor would this be the first time it has happened to Inner Mongolia. Once before, in 1928, Inner Mongolia was split up among several Chinese provinces, thus vanishing for a time from the map of China.

## One Nation, One Faith

It would have been most inconsistent and illogical if the persecution of the language and culture of the Mongols were not accompanied by similar attacks on their religion. As we expected from the start, the Chinese authorities did display a full measure of consistency and logic. Far back in the time of imperial China the Lamaist religion, the yellow faith of the Mongols, had been the target of savage repression and persecution. This is how the Mongols themselves described the situation in a letter to the Russian authorities: "In the seventeenth year of the rule of Guan-tsui the evil Chinese, putting on their so-called red hat, in many Hoshuns began beating up both the yellow (lamas) and the black (laymen), both old people and children, and to burn temples and monasteries, and villages, and to break holy images."

But imperial China was a haven of tolerance and benevolence, compared with Mao's China, especially during the Cultural Revolution. The drive to destroy religious shrines and persecute the faithful which rocked all the national regions of China made no exception of Inner Mongolia. The destruction of Buddhist temples and ancient monuments and the wholesale beating of priests and monks were accompanied by brutal propaganda attacks. Teng Hai-ching declared that the enemy "was using religion" to provoke disorders and "inflict harm on the great Cultural Revolution." In other words, the aim of official propaganda was to make religion synonymous with enemy. And the treatment meted out in China today to those labeled as enemies is too well known to require either elucidation or comment.

It would be unfair to assert, however, that the confrontation of church and secular authority was a problem relating only to Inner Mongolia. It will be recalled that in different periods of history it occurred—and still does—all over the world: in Western Europe, in Latin America, and in Asia. It is a process that could not fail to affect Outer Mongolia as well. As Owen Lattimore has written in this connection, "It is obvious that the Mongols of the twentieth century had either to modernise their society and state or perish as a people." On no account, however, was this process initiated by the "evil designs" of any Communist leader. Owen Lattimore has pointed out that, even if there had been no Marx or Lenin, modernization in the Mongolian People's Republic would have been impossible without a struggle between church and state, without social reform. The Mongols would otherwise have shared the fate of the Tasmanians or tribes like the Lennilappi Indians. The main problem is what forms this contest between two ideologies (secular and religious) will take. It may take the form of atheistic propaganda, as is the case in present-day Outer Mongolia. Or it may take the form of the barbarity and vandalism we are today witnessing in China.

In Ulan-Bator I visited the monastery of Gandang. Standing on top of a hill and surrounded by a high wall, the monastery is a well-known monument of Buddhist architecture. Some of the lamas are quite young. Young faces are to be seen among the worshippers who come here on days of prayer. They are the ones who, in choosing between the two forms of philosophy—the atheistic and the religious—have found the religious to be more convincing. I spoke to some of them.

"For me," one young novice said, "the path I have chosen is not something unexpected or contrary to my previous ideas and concepts. I am a historian by education." Indeed, I soon saw that for many young Mongols who turn to Buddhism this act is a way of expressing their devotion to the past rather than of repudiating the present. It is first and foremost an act of devotion to the national and cultural past of their people. In present-day Mongolia there are two ways in which you can serve that task: through religion or through historical research. In some aspects—the field of ethics for one—both these forms of activity come into contact. The scholar who deals with the history of Mongol Buddhism or with publication of ancient texts unwittingly finds himself influenced by the philosophical and ethical concepts that are the object of his study. In the same way, the lama who devotes himself to studying and interpreting the ancient texts is involuntarily playing the part of a scholar. This is why the degree of the influence of Buddhist philosophy on the modern Mongol intelligentsia defies precise analysis and calculation. The number of people present at official prayer meetings or monastery services offers the least convincing proof one way or another. Characteristically in the Mongolian People's Republic, the museums, which are repositories of the religious past, and the temples which are still in use are practically indistinguishable. For the museums are nothing but well-preserved, albeit inoperative, temples where the greatest care is taken to preserve ancient Buddhist texts, mandalas, religious statues, and images. The care lavished on all these attributes of the past invariably provokes the admiration of Buddhists from abroad who visit the Mongolian People's Republic individually or as members of various delegations. In recent years the number of foreign Buddhists visiting Mongolia has been growing steadily. To some extent this is due to Tibet's having been cut off from the family of Buddhist nations. Until Tibet's status, both internationally and in the Buddhist world, is restored, Mongolia is fast becoming the sole heir of its spiritual functions. This new status of Mongolia is today acquiring increasing recognition in the Buddhist church. One of the forms of that recognition is the large number of international gatherings and conferences of Buddhists whose venue is Ulan-Bator. Buddhists from Sri Lanka, India, Nepal, the Soviet Union, and Mongolia met at Ulan-Bator in December 1969. Another meeting took place in the summer of 1970. It was attended by delegations from ten countries: India, Japan, Ceylon, North and South Vietnam, Nepal, Malaysia, Singapore, and the Soviet Union. The conference decided to set up a special body, the Committee for the Cooperation of Asian Buddhists in the struggle for peace. Elected as its president was Bandido-Hamba Lama S. Gombozhav, a Mongol.

The Buddhists who travel to the Mongolian People's Republic from all over the world display a natural interest in the various treasures and relics of their faith. Among them is the residence of the last Bogdo-Gegen, the supreme lama of Mongolia, who died in 1924. After him no new Bogdo-Gegen was ever appointed to take his place; the leaders of the Mongolian People's Republic who decided to leave his residence empty were subsequently accused of "leftist extremism," relieved of their posts, and imprisoned. Some time later the authorities tried to restore the office of Bogdo-Gegen but the absence of unity among the leaders of the yellow religion in Mongolia made this impossible.

It was also in the 20s that the idea first appeared that the Panchen Lama should perhaps take over the spiritual leadership of Mongolia. Indeed, when he left Tibet in 1924, he did in fact take up residence in Inner Mongolia. Had he been bold enough to take over the leadership, as was most strongly rumored at the time that he would, it would have served not only to consolidate all Mongols under the symbol of the faith but also it would have served to strengthen the faith itself in this northernmost stronghold of Buddhism.

Of course at that time it was difficult to anticipate the subsequent course of events. Even assuming the then highly improbable eventuality of the Communists extending their rule to the whole of China, it would have been quite impossible to anticipate either the Cultural Revolution or the monstrous persecution of Lamaism in Tibet or the escape of the Dalai Lama from Tibet. But if at that time the Panchen Lama had accepted the role of Mongolia's religious leader, some of the recent events would undoubtedly have taken a different turn. It is certainly true that the Dalai Lama would have chosen a different route after leaving Tibet. It may fairly confidently be assumed that in this case Outer Mongolia, the land of the yellow religion, would have become his residence.

If this has not happened it is largely due to the efforts made by the Central Chinese Government. The Chinese colonial administration has always been well aware of the danger lurking in the possible rapprochement of Tibet and Mongolia. Not in vain has it constantly sought to block the slightest manifestation of this affinity and solidarity.

But, nevertheless, even under the present circumstances, the appearance of the Dalai Lama in Mongolia, if it ever occurred, would be an event that could become the turning point in the history of that nation. For one thing, it would result in a resurgence of religion in the Mongolian People's Republic. The monasteries and temples turned into museums would again resound with voices raised in prayer. The appearance on the scene of a multitude of believers would undoubtedly be a surprise for the Mongolian authorities. However, in all probability, the authorities would accept this. For it would imply the rebirth of yet another impetus, that of religion, for the unification of all Mongols. That, at any rate, is the way I see it.

Moreover, neither for the leaders of party nor religion would such a turn of events imply any departure from the previous line pursued by each of those two groups. In fact, it would mean continuing their former—and traditional—policy.

At this juncture it would be most appropriate to recall the principles underlying the sources of the Communist movement in Mongolia. The very first point in the party oath which was at one and the same time the statute and the program of the party read: "The aims of the People's Party of Outer Mongolia are to purge the country of the pernicious enemies harming the cause of the nation and of religion, to return the rights forfeited by Mongolia, to strengthen the state and religion."

So, the Mongolian Communists actually identified protection of the nation with protection of religion. The gradual return of the present leaders of the Mongolian People's Republic to that line would certainly have very far-reaching consequences. And they would be of particular significance in Asia for no enemy has inflicted so much harm on Asian Communists as their own avowed atheism. And ironically their atheism is very largely an act of mimicry whose origins are to be found in Moscow. As several Asian Communists have told me in private, in the present day world the drawing together of humanistic ideologies is a logical process. This is especially true today when it is a natural reaction to the opposing philosophy of "deideologization." Some efforts along these lines are being made by the Sri Lanka Communists and the Communists of India and Vietnam. Highly significant in this regard is the rise of Socialist ideology in the modern Arab world. It would also be relevant to recall the dialogue between Communists and Catholics in France and Italy which also attests to the universality of this phenomenon. Those Asian Communists who might venture further along this road would be showing an example for others to follow. And there is no reason why the Mongolian Communists should not be the ones to do so, the more so since this would not involve a departure from previous policies or tendencies, but dedication to them.

The same may be said of the Dalai Lama and his attitude toward

Mongolia. This too involves a return to existing traditions and precedents. In 1904 when Peking dethroned the Dalai Lama, the thirteenth Dalai Lama left Tibet and sought asylum in Mongolia. There, while in exile, he remained the religious ruler of Tibet which had never recognized Peking's unlawful act. And it was from Mongolia that the Dalai Lama once more returned in triumph to Lhasa.

These ties are preserved to this very day. In a June 1977 interview with the Indian weekly *Sunday*, the Dalai Lama told of his meeting with the Bogdo-Gegen of Mongolia at the Fifth Conference of Asian Buddhists in Delhi. "When we started to pray, and naturally I was saying my prayers in Tibetan, I found to my great surprise that the Bogdo-Gegen was using the same language. So I became convinced that the old ties between Tibet and these people are still very strong and make themselves felt."

# 3

# THE BUDDHA'S DISCIPLES LEARN TO FIGHT

### Tibet—The Country That Walked by Itself

A historical stone pillar has been preserved at Lhasa, the capital of Tibet. Its surface carries the inscribed text of a treaty concluded twelve centuries ago between the ruler of Tibet and the Chinese emperor. "No smoke or dust shall appear between the two countries. Not even those guarding the frontier shall feel apprehension or take fright. Land is land and bed is bed." The language is that of a treaty between equally independent and sovereign states. In the centuries that followed, as history wended its way through incredible zigzags, twists, and turns, Tibet alternated between Chinese vassal and independent state. As early as the nineteenth century Tibet had been waging wars of its own which had no bearing whatsoever on China, such as the war of 1841 with a Kashmirian prince and the war of 1856 with Nepal, as a result of which Tibet had to pay Nepal an annual tribute of 10,000 rupees. (The tribute was dutifully sent from Lhasa to Katmandu every year thereafter; for some time Tibet continued to pay it even after having been overrun by Mao's forces.) By the time of the collapse of imperial power in China, Tibet had moved further away from Peking than ever before.

51

Tibet's secession from China was recognized de facto by the European powers. Britain certainly demonstrated its attitude when it signed an agreement with Tibet which was later ratified at Simla in November 1904. Article 1 of the treaty read: "The government of Tibet engages to respect the Anglo-Chinese convention of 1890 and recognise the frontier between Sikkim and Tibet." It was thereby plainly stated that an agreement signed by Peking was on no account binding upon Lhasa and called for special confirmation to be valid.

So when the thirteenth Dalai Lama declared Tibet's independence in 1912, this was merely an act which formalized de jure a situation that had existed de facto.

Peking today disputes Tibet's right to that step. But if it wanted to be consistent Peking should likewise deny the independence of Nepal. For, like Tibet, Nepal broke away from China and formally declared its independence in 1923. But the time may well come when China will dispute that too.

Today Peking is contesting the Dalai Lama's rights. But who other than the Dalai Lama was the supreme ruler of Tibet? Characteristically, even the Ching emperors identified Tibet through its ruler and not the other way around. Hence their definition of Tibet as "the land of the Dalai Lama."

Challenging Tibet's right to independence, Peking is today invoking the 1914 agreement between Tibet and China. But that agreement, spearheaded as it was against British intrigues in Tibet, merely provided for Chinese patronage over Tibet while specifically emphasizing China's complete noninterference in Tibet's internal affairs. But, most important of all, the agreement was never signed by one of the contracting parties, namely China itself. Therefore, as an international document it has never actually entered into force. And anyway, the agreement omitted to describe Tibet as being a component part of China or to say anything about its incorporation into China.

From the declaration of independence to the occupation by Chinese soldiers in 1951, Tibet saw itself as an independent and sovereign state—and was seen as such by the outside world. In that capacity it maintained independent relations with the neighboring states of India and Nepal. And what other proof can there be of Tibet's sovereignty vis-á-vis China than the diplomatic relations that existed between

Peking and Lhasa which were suspended only in July 1949—on Tibet's initiative?

After the declaration of independence not a single Chinese soldier remained on Tibetan territory. According to a British consul who had been in Tibet, even isolated Chinese armed groups who ventured to accompany the occasional travelers into Tibetan territory were constantly sustaining losses from attacks upon them by Tibetan troops.

A member of a Soviet delegation which visited Tibet in 1922 recalled that from 1913 the boundary between Tibet and China was little more than a front line. There were frequent shooting incidents and skirmishes. The caravan routes from Tibet into China were blocked.

The six-man delegation of Kalmycks and Buryats was received by the Dalai Lama the day after their arrival in Tibet. In accordance with tradition, they presented him with gifts from the Soviet government: one hundred arshins of brocade, four gold watches, a silver tea set, and a radio telegraphic apparatus. This piece of equipment aroused particular interest.

"Is Russia strong?" the Dalai Lama's ministers wanted to know. "Can Russia help Tibet and protect it from encroachments by other states?"

The delegation assured the ministers that Tibet could fully rely on Russia's support and assistance. Outside support in the struggle against China must indeed have been very important for Lhasa for the Dalai Lama promptly dispatched his secretary to Moscow with a personal message.

This reaction to the prospects of receiving aid from outside is symptomatic. According to the already mentioned British consul, there then existed in Tibet a well-defined "nationalist school, intolerant of the Chinese connection and in favour of bringing the ethnological and political frontiers of Tibet together by force of arms, of recovering from China all Tibetan-inhabited territory still in her hands."

Throughout the four decades of Tibet's independence the relations between Tibet and China were those of two independent and poorly associated states. Furthermore, the question of Tibet's return to the Chinese fold was never raised, except, of course, for a few statements by Nanking which purely theoretically declared, among other things, Tibet's inalienability from China. The unilateral statements were simply ignored by Lhasa.

In refusing to recognize Tibet's independence, Nanking was pursuing the same line as with Outer Mongolia whose independence it just as stubbornly refused to recognize for thirty-five years. In both cases the Chinese government went no further than statements. It wisely refrained from the action which declarations of this kind would seem to call for. One such statement indirectly confirming the nonrecognition of Tibet's independence was that made by Chiang Kai-shek in August 1945 promising independence "if and when the Tibetans attain the stage of complete self-reliance in political and economic conditions."

On the other hand, statements of this kind may be regarded as indirect evidence of Tibet's factual secession. For if that were not the case, such statements could not have been made at all. After all, no one would venture to assert or try to prove that California is a part of the United States or that London is an inalienable part of England. Statements of this kind can only be made as antitheses of contradictory assertions.

As in the case of the other national territories of China, Mao's government fully and unalterably inherited the colonial line of the preceding Chinese governments. "Tibet," the Peking government declared in its note of October 30, 1950, "is an integral part of Chinese territory. The problem of Tibet is entirely a domestic problem of China."

No one can say what the possible repercussions of the Communist Chinese attempt to occupy Tibet might have been had Peking and Taipei not caught the world unawares by their show of complete solidarity on that issue. To quote from an American publication, "When the UN seemed likely to be invoked, it was found that Chiang Kai-shek was just as firm as Mao Tse-tung on the question, and the matter was dropped." [1]

---

[1] From *The Modern History of China* by H. Mealeavy, published in New York in 1967, p. 352.

populated. Efforts must be made to raise the population from the present level of two million . . . . to more than 10 million."

The far-reaching aims of this policy, too, were, of course, formulated in Peking. They were voiced with absolute lucidity by Mao Tse-tung in his speech at a reception honoring the Dalai Lama and the Panchen Lama on September 20, 1954. The aims of China with regard to Tibet, Mao declared, are to populate it with Chinese immigrants in a proportion of five to one in respect to the local population.

As in the other national areas, the influx of Chinese immigrants is paralleled by an extensive drive to assimilate the local population. In the words of the Dalai Lama, it is a program of "sinification." The identical methods applied in carrying out this policy not only in Tibet but also in Mongolia, Sinkiang, and, earlier, in Manchuria confirms the belief that Peking has elaborated a single nationwide program for the assimilation of the non-Han peoples. As in the other areas, the very first targets of the assimilation drive in Tibet were the national language and local religion.

In Tibetan primary schools the children may now use their own language only during the first two years. Starting with the third year tuition is only in Chinese. Chinese is also the official language in Tibet.

The natural opposition of the local people and their attempts to resist collapse on contact with the iron inflexibility of the administrative bureaucracy which is supported, as soon as the situation gets out of control, by the machine-gun fire of Chinese soldiers.

The best way to suppress a nation's will to resist is to dismember it. This is the method that was applied to Tibet. Not all Tibetans have been included within the boundaries of the Tibetan autonomous region. Other Tibetan-inhabited areas, though directly adjacent to Tibet, have nonetheless been administratively incorporated in various other Chinese provinces. These Tibetan lands which have been purposefully and deliberately torn away from Tibet are fairly extensive. Altogether they make up nine autonomous districts.

Religious persecution began in Tibet even before the Cultural Revolution. But it was the Red Guards who completed the ruin of the spiritual world of the Tibetans, leaving shrines reduced to rubble and ancient manuscripts in ashes.

Hundreds of Red Guards supported by Chinese militia armed with machine guns broke into the holy of holies, the great temple of Jokhang at Lhasa. This was the signal. It set off a frenzy of vandalism which culminated in the destruction of the finest achievements of Tibetan culture of the last two thousand years. With shrieks and howls of joy the Red Guards hurled statues down from their pedestals, tore down sacred images, and burned ancient manuscripts and paintings. The long list of sacred Buddhist shrines overrun and defiled by the Red Guards includes the monasteries of Tangya Ling and Ramo-chi. According to the Dalai Lama, the Chinese have completely destroyed all Buddhist shrines and monasteries.

Destruction of the material attributes of religion was accompanied by a no less concerted campaign to eliminate the servants of religion. Again according to the Dalai Lama, not one of the 300,000 Tibetan monks is still in Tibet today. "At present," notes a Soviet observer, "virtually no temporal or religious leader of the Tibetan people is still at liberty."

Even those isolated and fragmentary facts which come to light through refugees are sufficient to provide a general picture of the tragedy that has overtaken Tibet. An entire nation has been placed at the mercy of a foreign colonial machine which has deliberately set out to destroy or assimilate it. As a result, according to the *Daily Telegraph*, the Tibetan population has dropped by 200,000. The Dalai Lama was not exaggerating when he declared that the Tibetan race was threatened with total extinction or that, if the present situation in Tibet continues, its people face the menace of complete annihilation.

Yet this tragedy with all its horror and violence had to happen before the Tibetans could bring themselves, contrary to the spirit of traditional Buddhist docility, to take up arms and rise in a desperate and hopeless struggle against the Chinese colonial monster. In the words of the Dalai Lama, the Tibetan people are not fighting against any particular social or political system. Tibet "may even become a Communist state. The Tibetans are fighting against foreign domination and their aim is the restoration of Tibet's independence."

The present-day situation in China gives her leaders convenient ground to dissociate themselves from many things that were done during Mao's rule, in particular from what was done to the Tibetans. Accusing the "gang of four" of distorting the nationalities policy, which is what the crimes perpetrated against the non-Han peoples are now called, today's leaders of China make a double gain. On the one hand they proclaim their nonparticipation in all deeds that provoked the dissatisfaction and hatred of the national minorities, while on the other, they do not relinquish any part of their share in all that has been achieved as a result of carrying out this policy. Thus, Hua Ko-feng and his followers, giving nothing away that has been done to achieve assimilation and national unity of the country, are releasing a safety valve for the accumulated dissatisfaction by laying the very same "gang of four" open to the critics' fire.

## Buddhists Up in Arms

The self-imposed exile of the reigning Dalai Lama sets no precedent. When Tibet declared its independence from China in 1912 the Dalai Lama also had to flee from his country to save his life. While in exile he remained Tibet's secular and religious ruler and his orders and instructions were still law. On one occasion the abbot of a lamasery asked him for advice. Some Chinese soldiers led by a captain had entered the lamasery and he wanted to know what to do. The reply of the docile Dalai Lama, the vice-regent and incarnation of the en-lightened Buddha, was, "If they are stronger than we, try and expel them with the help of kind words. But if you are stronger, cut them down."

The Tibetans are following that rule to this day. Every time they see they are stronger than the Chinese occupation forces, they lose no opportunity to cut them down.

At first, the Chinese colonial administrators tried to explain the hostility of the local people, which developed into armed resistance at the slightest provocation, by "a serious lack of mutual understanding between nations." The nations in question were, of course, the Han Chinese and the Tibetans, This at any rate was how General Chang Ching-wu interpreted it in 1955 in his report to the State Council. In his own words, "This resulted in lack of understanding and doubts among some Tibetan personnel, which in turn hindered the smooth progress of our work."

Later, when the armed resistance assumed a mass scale such explanations could no longer hold water. In 1959 the insurgents gained control over southern Tibet and to put down the unrest the regular Chinese army had to mount a massive offensive.

Organized resistance continued even after the suppression of the principal centers of revolt. The gravity of the situation, even as late as 1965, is illustrated by an attempt by a 25,000-strong rebel force to capture Lhasa.

The never-ending colonial war flared up anew during the Cultural Revolution. Taking advantage of the struggle between rival Chinese groups, the Tibetans captured large quantities of arms and ammunition. According to the information trickling out of Tibet, all this hardware has not been lying idle. In a dispatch from India in late 1969 an Associated Press correspondent indicated that Tibetan guerrilla groups were becoming so active that, fearing for their lives, the Chinese were compelled to travel in large groups.

The massive scale of Tibetan resistance was also evidenced by the massive scale of Chinese reprisals. The methods were almost the same as those used by the Nazis during World War II—though without much success. The Chinese began applying their punitive measures almost immediately after the much-vaunted "liberation" of Tibet. As early as the summer of 1956 a group of Tibetans led by the Dalai Lama's brother launched an appeal to world public opinion through Jawaharlal Nehru on account of the killing of 4000 peaceful civilians during the punitive bombing of Litang village by the Chinese air force. According to unofficial reports, between March 1959 and September 1960, 87,000 Tibetans were killed, 25,000 were arrested, and 80,000 fled from the country. In other words, one-sixth of the population was affected by the reprisals.

Judging by the continuous stream of reports about reprisals in Tibet, what is going on in the country is not just some isolated campaign or system of campaigns, it is a system of relationships between colonial authorities and the local population. This view certainly seems to be borne out by reports of continuing public executions in Lhasa and other areas of Tibet and accounts of mass purges throughout the country. In the summer and autumn of 1970 Tibetan towns and villages were plastered with enlarged photographs and posters showing Tibetans who had been sentenced in absentia to death or to imprisonment for as long as twenty or thirty years. The pictures of those sentenced to death are marked with a big red cross. Refugees who have been lucky enough to escape have testified that equally represented in this death-row gallery are local leaders and former feudals as well as those usually styled by official Peking propaganda as "liberated slaves and paupers."

There are two striking things about this account. The first is the number of portraits, which provides additional proof of the scale of resistance. The second is the fact that they have all been sentenced in their absence. This seems to show that the Chinese administration is powerless to carry out the sentences it has passed. In all probability the culprits have either fled from Tibet or else—for the most part—are hiding out in the mountains with the numerous combat units that are ceaselessly harassing the Chinese occupation forces. One of the strongholds of these national armed forces is on Chemogangar Mountain. The Central News Agency has reported from Taipei that central Tibet is at present controlled by those forces. Another stronghold is in the area of Mount Kualan where a 3000-strong Tibetan detachment has been based for some time.

On November 15, 1969, Agency France Presse reported from Taipei that in one operation these forces killed over a thousand Chinese soldiers. In another operation in the Tsianba area 200 Chinese lost their lives. Another 300 Chinese soldiers were killed during the Tibetan attack on Nehalma. Two hundred and fifty more were killed during an attack on the Chinese garrison at Setang, 70 miles from Lhasa. The list can be continued almost endlessly.

According to subsequent reports, Tibetan resistance is continuing. In July 1970 the pro-Chinese Radio Lhasa reported an armed uprising in central Tibet. It qualified the rebels as a "handful of class enemies." Commenting on another mutiny, this time in western Tibet in October 1970, Radio Lhasa went out of its way to explain that it was all the work of a "miserable bunch of class enemies."

It requires no mental effort to realize that if all this opposition was merely the work of a "handful" or a "bunch," Peking would have no need to keep a 40,000-strong army in Tibet. At any rate, most foreign observers of the Chinese scene assess the armed forces of fighting Tibet in categories very different from "handful" or "bunch." According to figures relating to the early phase of the anti-China movement, twenty-three guerrilla detachments in eastern and sixteen in southern Tibet were believed to total something like 100,000 to 200,000 men.

The real strength, perhaps, even invincibility, of Tibet's resistance is not merely in the numbers of men who have today taken up arms or made for the mountains. Ultimately, Tibet's liberation movement may well prove to be invincible because, in the words of Radio Lhasa, many people "try to rebel against the new regime at the very first opportunity."

These words, uttered by a Tibetan announcer on a Chinese radio program posing as the "Voice of Lhasa," objectively and succinctly describe the situation in Tibet today. Armed resistance by the insurgents is an almost continuous process. And it would not take much more than a small spark to kindle the flame of a mass uprising. Naturally enough Peking is very careful not to let the sparks fly. And just as naturally Peking will never accept the Dalai Lama's suggestion that a free and fair plebiscite be held in Tibet. A plebiscite of this kind—and its rejection too for that matter—might well become that spark. The Dalai Lama's proposal made in March 1975 may surely be expected to have some far-reaching consequences for the future of Tibet.

The reprisals have never ceased. In 1972, for instance, 12,000 people were killed during the suppression of just one out of a whole series of rebellions. The tens of thousands of wounded, imprisoned, and exiled are countless.

# 4

# THE GREAT
# HOSTAGE

## Yellow Colonialism

The usual Soviet image conjured up by the word "colonizer" is that of a white man in a sun helmet with a switch in his hand.

Yet this typically Kiplingesque character will evoke no associations in the minds of many colonial peoples. Many millions of people in the East are familiar with a completely different kind of colonizer: the silk-gowned Han with his pigtail and long bamboo stick. This is the kind of man associated with the word "colonizer" in the minds of the people of Sinkiang, one of the oldest colonies of China.

The name Sinkiang is of Chinese origin and dates back to the time of the Chinese conquest. In Chinese it means New Frontier. After the establishment of Communist rule in China the Uighurs made an attempt to get the name abolished because of its colonial overtones. But the Peking regime vetoed the proposal and qualified it as a manifestation of "bourgeois nationalism." For the purposes of this book, however, I intend to use the territory's traditional name which is Eastern Turkestan. All the more so since even today, and in spite of the ban, most of the people living in the territory are still calling it by that very name.

The fact that Sinkiang, or Eastern Turkestan, has been an economic colony of China since its conquest is well known. It has been defined as such by all Soviet researchers, not only in recent years but also at the time when the sun of Sino-Soviet friendship was at its zenith.

Characteristically, Eastern Turkestan was always governed in true colonial fashion, with Chinese (or Manchu) in positions of the highest authority and representatives of the local nobility in the lower echelons of power.

Toward the end of the imperial period of its history China itself was a semicolonial territory. It was indeed a China of foreign concessions and European settlements, a country cringing in fear of the European gunboats patrolling its shores. All this is true for it is a part of history. But it is equally true that at the same time China played the part of colonialist in Manchuria, Mongolia, Tibet, and Eastern Turkestan.

The situation was reminiscent of a feudal hierarchy when a vassal was at the same time lord to his own vassals. On the one hand, China was a semicolony; on the other, a colonial power.

Regretfully, the first definition has almost completely overshadowed the second one. Of the two Chinas—China the victim and China the colonialist—only the first is generally known while "yellow" colonialism, one of the most appalling forms of Asian colonialism, has until very recently been largely overlooked.

A. Screen, a British consul who visited Eastern Turkestan in the 1920s, wrote down his impressions, emphasizing the insistence with which the Chinese had for ages asserted their claim to Eastern Turkestan. He recalled that in spite of the distances involved (even in his time the journey from Peking to Kashgar took about five months), entire Chinese armies were dispatched, if necessary, to the western frontiers.

Considering the enduring and most vigorous interest taken in this area by Britain, which was even farther away, the consul's amazement may perhaps have been a bit incongruous, but that is beside the point.

Conquered by Peking in 1759, Eastern Turkestan became one of China's biggest colonies. Equal in size to East and West Germany together, it makes up almost one-fifth of China's entire territory.

Although precise data on the deposits and extraction of mineral resources constitute a military secret in present-day China, it is certainly no secret that this area is rich in oil. It also accounts for a sizable portion of the coal mined in China today. Not least in importance is the fact that China's nuclear testing ground is also in Eastern Turkestan. It is there, in the desert of Lop Nor, that the disciples of the Great Helmsman, Mao, are developing the weapons that are to clear the way for what they regard as "world revolution." In present-day China this term is used as a euphemism for the unbridled territorial expansion that began in the earliest period of Chinese history and has continued ever since. Eastern Turkestan is but one of the stages in that expansion.

## Rebels With a Cause

There are probably no other people in the world who have fought so stubbornly for their independence as those of Eastern Turkestan. The nineteenth and twentieth centuries constitute an endless chain of colonial wars waged by the Chinese forces in that territory.

Hardly had the insurrection of 1814 been suppressed when two years later a new one broke out. A decade went by and in 1826 Turkestan was again the scene of bitter fighting. This time in order to quell the uprising the Chinese overlords had to bring in from China proper a 100,000-strong force—an army unparalleled in size for its time. Suffice it to say that the British colonial army controlling the whole of India comprised no more than 30,000 men.

The suppression of that uprising provoked an exodus akin to that of the Israelites from Egypt. Several thousand people fled from Eastern Turkestan to Central Asia to escape the vengeance of the Chinese.

New outbursts of insurrection then followed one upon the other in 1830, 1847, 1857, and 1864. These were but the peak years of insurrections and of the punitive colonial expeditions that followed in their wake.

According to one eyewitness account dating back to the 1860s, "everywhere the population, armed with anything that came to hand, destroyed Chinese garrisons and slew Chinese officials and usurers. In some cases even native officials were killed if they had been too zealous in promoting the interests of the Chinese administration."

The Russian traveler G.E. Grum-Grzhimailo, who visited Eastern

Turkestan somewhat later, has also given an account of the unceasing colonial wars in Eastern Turkestan. In 1862–1863, he writes, "the Chinese were placed in a desperate situation. Many thousands of them perished, but then, step by step, in the next 13 years they put down the rebellion."

These thirteen years of anticolonial war prove two things: the indomitable determination of Eastern Turkestan to achieve independence and the equally strong determination of China to hold on to that territory at any cost.

Mahatma Gandhi's well-known dictum that violence can only beget violence may be illustrated very convincingly by the example of Eastern Turkestan. Instead of pacifying the area, every new Chinese punitive operation provoked more and more insurrection. "The presence of Chinese troops in this region," wrote the Russian explorer Nikolai Przhevalsky (of horse fame) after a visit to Eastern Turkestan, "serves not to pacify it, but constitutes an inexhaustible source of looting and all manner of oppression of the local population. At the same time the entire farming population has been subjected to exorbitant and ruthlessly exacted taxation."

The defeat of the uprising and the subsequent reprisals once again prompted many people to flee in the opposite direction, within the Russian Empire. For instance, the population of the Kuldja count emigrated almost to a man. Grum-Grzhimailo described an incident on the frontier river, Horgos, in which a Cossack unit covered "the rear of a crowd of many thousand natives emigrating into our territory."

The irreconcilable relationship between the Chinese colonial administration and the local population was commented on by virtually all foreign travelers in the area—from the high-ranking Russian imperial official in Siberia, I.F. Babkov, to Grum-Grzhimailo and later travelers, including Westerners. "The native population regarded the Chinese with hatred," wrote Grum-Grzhimailo in his diary, "and only fear of Chinese arms could keep the natives in submission." The implacable antagonism between the local people and the colonial administration which permeated the entire history of the area was also noted by the British scholar B. Davidson, who visited Eastern Turkestan in the 1950s: "Rebellion and repression," he wrote, "had followed hard on one another's heels, and gradually this whole vast region became an emptiness on the world's map."

Colonial authorities usually tend to fight shy of publicizing any unrest that occurs in areas under their rule—except of course for cases when suppression of the unrest may be interpreted as a praiseworthy exploit. The Chinese colonial empire was no exception to the rule. One of the few known departures was the publication in Shanghai in 1952 of *Documents on the Uprising of the Moslems* in four volumes. Characteristically, the two final volumes were entirely devoted to the uprisings in Eastern Turkestan and their quelling by the Chinese troops.

This publication was most probably due to an oversight on the part of the Peking authorities. Since then all publications dealing with attempts by the minority peoples of China to achieve their independence have been banned by Peking.

The longing for independence has continued to exist nonetheless. It has survived all the punitive measures with their corollary of purely Chinese ruthlessness. The years 1911–1912 were marked by new uprisings in Eastern Turkestan. And as before many of the local inhabitants continued to seek refuge in neighboring Russia. In 1905, a relatively tranquil year, 14,000 refugees arrived in Ferghana alone from Eastern Turkestan and in 1908 the number rose to 28,000.

According to some accounts, 70,000 Kazakhs, Uighurs, and Dunganians escaped from Eastern Turkestan to Central Asia. The Russian government took a lenient view of this influx of refugees. "In the last decade," A. Kokhanovsky noted, "besides the Dunganians and Taranchians, no small number of Kirghiz have emigrated to Russia from Western China, partially with imperial consent."

Such pro-Russian sentiments in Eastern Turkestan became a kind of tradition. This has been emphasized by several Russian scholars and explorers, including Przhevalsky. Owen Lattimore also stressed that "the Central Asian people had always tended to accord prestige and admiration more readily to Russia than to China."

The uprisings of 1911–1912 were followed by the insurrection of 1941. An eyewitness wrote: "In 1931 there began at Ham a big Uighur revolt that was to signal nearly 20 years of repression and renewed uprising. After 1931, there was no more peace in Sinkiang."

The troops sent in by the central government acted in the traditional manner: "On this day and the next, in a house-to-house visitation, some 2,000 or 3,000 persons were slain, mostly with swords so as to save ammunition. Many of those killed were unarmed old men, as well as women and children."

## Two Generals: Between Moscow and Peking

There are some pages in the history book of Sino-Soviet relations that defy traditional logic. Such for instance is the story of General Ma. General Ma, who was sent by the Central Chinese Government to pacify Eastern Turkestan, sustained a defeat. His army was routed and he was compelled to flee. Going by the rules of the game, he should have rushed back into the arms of the government that had sent him. But General Ma did not appear in China.

At a pinch, he could have fled to India, where he could probably have found asylum. But General Ma did not appear in India either.

General Ma fled to Moscow.

This militarist and colonialist, "whose hands were steeped in the blood of the working people," as the Soviet papers had described him, quietly settled down in one of the government dachas just outside Moscow.

With him were his aides and retinue. The general had a car and security guard placed at his disposal. In the evenings, dressed in a civilian suit tailor-made for him in one of the Kremlin's special tailoring establishments, he enjoyed making appearances at concerts or theater performances in Moscow. The "bloody hatchet-man of Turkestan" suddenly revealed a passionate love of revolutionary plays by Soviet authors. He was rumored to have been received in the highest Soviet circles and to have had confidential talks.

In terms of traditional logic this situation defies a rational explanation. Forgiveness and charitability toward a fallen class enemy may perhaps be a splendid virtue. But it was certainly never included in the long list of virtues attributed to Stalin. What then could he have had in mind when he took that far-reaching step?

The keys to many problems of present-day China are to be found in its past. Likewise, the secret goal pursued by Stalin should be sought outside this particular situation and in situations similar to it.

Some of these situations date back to the period of the revolution in Russia. There was at that time a man called Grigory Kotovsky, a famous leader of Bessarabian bandits and a convicted criminal. Yet no sooner did he accept the Communist creed than he became a hero of the Civil War and a general in the Red Army.

There was also a man called Makhno, a killer and the idol of Ukrainian nationalists. At one time he seemed to be throwing in his lot with the Communists. Lenin promptly began sending him letters, arms, and commissars who were supposed to convert him finally to the true faith. Had they succeeded, Makhno would have been listed in modern Soviet history books among the heroes of the Civil War and the revolution, and he would have been honored as Grigory Kotovsky is today.

In all probability, the Russian leaders regarded General Ma as being another such potential political leader. Perhaps even then the perspicacious Stalin regarded him as the possible alternative to Mao, whom he had never really trusted and never liked. The fact that during his stay in the Soviet Union General Ma not only studied the Russian language but also perused the classics of Marxism-Leninism certainly seems to provide a clue to the prospective political career for which he was being groomed in Moscow.

As for Stalin's attitude to Mao, the following episode provides ample illustration. One day, during Mao's protracted visit to the Soviet Union in 1950, Stalin was told that Mao Tse-tung had come to pay a call on him.

"What Mao Tse-tung?" Stalin queried probably, relishing the look of surprise that came over his secretary Poskrebyshev's face.

"Comrade Mao Tse-tung," Poskrebyshev explained. "The Chairman of the Communist Party of China."

"There is no Communist Party in China," Stalin countered, "only a group of Social Revolutionaries (SRs), who call themselves Communists."

This exchange was followed by a talk between Stalin and Mao Tse-tung which the Soviet press subsequently described as having passed in an atmosphere of "fraternal friendship" and "mutual understanding." This event was later reflected in the well-known painting "The

Great Friendship," where Stalin and Mao Tse-tung are depicted engaged in a cordial conversation during which, by the look of things, they are resolving the problems relating to the destinies of the world and the future of mankind. The great event was also translated into music, in the song "Moscow–Peking" which at that time used to be broadcast endlessly and sung at all meetings, rallies, and demonstrations. Its chorus seemed to have a particularly ominous and threatening meaning: "Stalin and Mao are listening to us, yes they are listening to us."

That Stalin, who disliked and mistrusted Mao, went out of his way to put on such a show of affinity indicates the lengths to which he was prepared to go for the sake of political expediency. But his desire to engineer the appearance in China of another political leader who could offset, eclipse, and finally oust the ambitious boss of the Chinese SRs who had usurped the title of Communist was even stronger. In the 1930s one such prospective leader was General Ma.

However, the best is the enemy of the good and nowhere is this saying so apt as in love and in politics. It was natural, therefore, that as soon as another more powerful figure appeared the Russian leaders began to lose interest in General Ma. And it was again in Eastern Turkestan that this new figure appeared.

But General Ma could not complain that no one in Moscow wanted to have anything more to do with him. By no means. As his importance in terms of the Kremlin's objectives dwindled, so more and more interest was displayed in him by the secret police. Endowed with a keen sense of time, they were always the first to divine when their moment had come.

In the deep of the night, several limousines rolled up to General Ma's house with their headlights dimmed. When several minutes later they drove out of the grounds, the career of the general, who could today have been the head of China's Communist government, was over.

Sheng Shih-tsai, another Chinese general and actually General Ma's successor, came somewhat closer to that objective.

The British scholar B. Davidson formulates the tasks facing the new Chinese governor in Eastern Turkestan thus: "His problem, essentially, was to combine the maintenance of Chinese rule with concessions to growing nationalism among the non-Chinese peoples of the country, and primarily among the Uighurs and Kazakhs. Sheng understood this."

Sheng did indeed and he was fully aware that in the situation prevailing in Turkestan at the time he could not hope to ride out the storm relying entirely upon local forces. The most logical step would have been to seek support in China, from whence he had been sent. But this Sheng Shih-tsai did not do. Instead he reached the conclusion that Eastern Turkestan was nearer to Moscow than to Nanking, politically if not geographically.

Having made his choice, Sheng began by establishing the broadest possible contacts with Soviet foreign-trade and economic organizations. In 1934, for instance, Russian geologists carried out an extensive survey throughout Eastern Turkestan. They drew up detailed maps of mineral resources, especially oil deposits. Soviet foreign-trade organizations were granted an oil-export monopoly. The agreement was in force until 1943, for over ten years. In 1940 another agreement was signed for the joint extraction of mineral resources, notably zinc, and for the building of communication facilities by Soviet experts.

It is highly characteristic that these agreements were signed not only without the approval of the central Chinese government, but also even without prior consultations with it. Moreover, when in 1935 Moscow granted Eastern Turkestan a loan of five million gold rubles, the Chinese government attempted to veto the arrangement—but in vain. As Chiang Kai-shek was to write later, "The Chinese government's efforts to prevent the loan proved in vain."

"Funds from the Soviet loans," writes Owen Lattimore, "were used to build more motor roads, and trucks in use increased from about 20 in 1933 to 400 in 1938 and eventually to 3,000 in 1941. In the same period 1,350 miles of telephone lines were installed. By 1939, there were some 20 factories in the province, and over 400 tons of Soviet machinery had gone into the construction of a refinery at an oilfield northwest of Urumchi."

It must have been no easy matter to obtain such generous aid from a country that was then only beginning to develop its own industry and which was acutely short of everything, from consumer goods to coal and steel. So the fact that Sheng nonetheless received the aid affirms two points: firstly, the importance attached by the Soviet leaders to the region, or rather to everything that could bolster its independence vis-à-vis China, and secondly, Sheng Shih-tsai's own political abilities. Of course, after all his contacts with Moscow he could hardly have expected to win any laurels in Nanking but probably he never did anyway. For the moment he was more than compensated by the understanding and appreciation that his talents had won him in Moscow.

In 1938 General Sheng Shih-tsai was invited to the Soviet Union. Characteristically, in accepting the invitation, Sheng made no attempt to consult the Nanking government and did not even notify it of his intentions. To the Chinese ambassador accredited to Moscow, Sheng's appearance at diplomatic receptions came as a complete and unpleasant surprise. In other words, Sheng comported himself (with Moscow's ready support) as head of a sovereign state having no more in common with China than with Guatemala or Canada.

Though his visit to Moscow was attended by no publicity, the general was treated with the utmost courtesy. He saw Molotov and Voroshilov and was received by Stalin. One of the results of his talk with Stalin was the stepping up of Russian arms deliveries to Eastern Turkestan. On this point Sheng had been particularly insistent for he knew the history of the area only too well. Every time Eastern Turkestan had displayed a desire for secession in the past, the Chinese army had inevitably come in to reshackle the colony to China, shedding rivers of blood in the process. While Mao Tse-tung and Chiang Kai-shek were fighting for control over Mainland China, they were both much too hard pressed to think about Eastern Turkestan. For some time this alone saved Sheng. But the first thing either of them would do as soon as the battle for control had been won would be to send the disengaged armies to attack Turkestan. This was in fact what happened but General Sheng had anticipated such an outcome.

Apart from the arms deliveries, Sheng Shih-tsai's meeting with Stalin had another result: During their talk Sheng raised the question of his membership in the Communist party of China.

"I am a devoted follower of Marxism–Leninism," he said. "In 1937 I submitted my application for membership in the CPC."

The Politbureau of the Chinese Communist party had unanimously approved but postponed the final decision until having consulted with the ruling body within the international Communist movement at that time. This was the Chinese form of a categoric but polite refusal. Mao

Tse-tung did not want a rival in the party who could compete with him in the power struggle in China.

Stalin promised to help Sheng become a Communist not only by conviction but also formally in the sense of full membership. Stalin kept his promise—though not quite in the way Sheng Shih-tsai had expected.

Before he left Moscow, Sheng was presented with a membership card of the Communist party of the Soviet Union bearing the number 1859118. Sheng had no option but to accept it with gratitude.

Moscow thereby killed two birds with one stone. Firstly, it inflicted a fairly resounding political slap in the face of Mao Tse-tung. And secondly, as a Soviet Communist, Sheng Shih-tsai now became formally subservient to the Central Committee of the party he had joined which was centered in Moscow.

Stalin had again carried off a masterly and farsighted coup. The fact that the Communist party of the Soviet Union, which was then completely infallible in the eyes of all Communists, had deigned to accept within its ranks a man who had been rejected by Mao's group could at the right time become a serious charge against Mao.

However, in Mao Stalin certainly met his match. There was no need to be either "great" or "wise" to feel the threat emanating from Eastern Turkestan. There was the danger of separatism which threatened to split China like a dropped watermelon. And it was a danger emanating personally from Sheng who, now that he had become a Communist with Moscow's help, could aspire to a position of leadership in the Communist movement in China. But if Sheng had become Mao's potential rival, Mao now took care to ensure that Sheng too should have a rival. The situation was reminiscent of the traditional Chinese ivory ball within a ball within a ball. To this end, Mao sent his own brother, Mao Tse-minh, to Eastern Turkestan to offset Sheng's influence there.

With Germany's attack on Russia, Stalin was forced to turn his attentions away from Eastern Turkestan. Forsaken by his protector, Sheng found himself face to face with Mao Tse-tung and his group. Shrewdly playing upon the separatist and nationalist feelings of local leaders, Mao Tse-minh managed to undermine Sheng's position. He rejoiced in his success, unaware that he was digging his own grave.

Sensing the threat to his authority, Sheng decided to do an about-face. Repudiating his former gods, he now swore allegiance to Nanking. But the gods in Nanking were thirsting for a sacrifice. It is not hard to guess who was to become that sacrifice. On a sudden order by Sheng all the Chinese Communists who had been sent to Turkestan by the Chinese Communist party were arrested and shot. And the first name on the death list was that of Mao's brother Mao Tse-minh.

Having thus settled his account with the past, Sheng promptly restored his long-lost ties with Chiang Kai-shek. The game that had been played out for so many years was now over. As for Sheng himself, having left the arena where he had been the star attraction for so long, the ex-dictator accepted the post of forestries minister at Nanking. Weary of fighting his way through the political jungles, he decided to find solace in the natural forests.

In summing up, perhaps it should be asked: Who took advantage of whom? Sheng of the Soviets with whose assistance he had hoped to extend his authority to the rest of the country or the Soviets of Sheng on whose back they had hoped to ride into China. I would venture to say that it is only in the cavalry corps that the position of horse and rider is clear. In other spheres, however, particularly the sphere of politics, the rider and the one who is ridden change places so frequently during the march that it is at times almost impossible to see which is the prevalent situation. And as often as not it is quite impossible to predict the direction of their movement and the objective they will reach. This is certainly true of Eastern Turkestan and the destinies of the political leaders appearing from time to time on its horizon.

What ultimate good, if any, did Sheng's rule do Eastern Turkestan? An attempt to provide a simple answer to that question would lead us into the realm of contradictions and paradoxes or into what Marxist philosophers call a "denial of a denial."

It will be recalled that the independent economic policy pursued by Sheng Shih-tsai was supported by an equally independent foreign policy. And the central Chinese government was powerless not only to govern this nominal province of China, but also even to influence its affairs. According to Sheng himself, the Nanking government would have been powerless to unseat him even if it had wanted to. "Little by little," writes Basil Davidson, "he removed Sinkiang from all but nominal loyalty to a China now more and more riven by the warlord wars. He would let in nobody across the borders of whom he did not personally approve, and let out nobody of whom he disapproved. He issued his own currency and made his own trade agreement with the emergent Soviet state."

There are several facts which show with particular clarity how far removed Eastern Turkestan was from China in those years. Thus, when in August 1942 Madame Chiang Kai-shek went to Turkestan to carry out an extremely delicate mission on behalf of her husband, her job included convincing Sheng of the need to "return to the national fold."

Chiang Kai-shek was later to describe the restoration by Sheng of ties with the central government as "the importance of preserving China's sovereignty and the necessity of returning the administrative authority of Sinkiang to the government."

Yet this drawing away on no account implied the final breakaway of Eastern Turkestan from China. What is more, it precluded it. In this connection an analogy may be drawn from family life. In husband–wife relations two principles are usually possible: the principle of the short leash or the principle of the long leash. The short leash, with which less astute wives try to keep their husbands at their sides, is the one most frequently broken. What Sheng Shih-tsai chose may be termed "the principle of the long leash." While acquiring an economic and political autonomy such as it had never enjoyed since becoming a Chinese colony, Eastern Turkestan did not, however, come any closer to real independence or to a real possibility of seceding from China. By publishing newspapers in the local languages and by sending hundreds of Uighurs and Kazakhs to study in the Soviet Union, Sheng blunted the national question. In this way he poured oil on the troubled waters of separatism in Eastern Turkestan. This was the meaning behind the "principle of the long leash." Thanks to his strategy the problem of Turkestan's secession from China was never even mentioned in all those years, in marked contrast to the preceding period and to the years that followed Sheng's rule.

In other words, Eastern Turkestan, which Sheng had seemed to be leading toward independence, was in fact led to the opposite goal, that is, of course, if independence is understood not as some token autonomy but as political secession and independent statehood.

To lead a country toward one goal and then in reality to bring it to the opposite goal is an example of political art that any politician can envy.

For that matter, Eastern Turkestan under Sheng could never have achieved anything more than it did. An independent Eastern Turkestan headed by a Chinese would have been just as nonsensical as an independent India headed by Lord Mountbatten or an independent Algeria headed by the French premier.

That is one side of the paradox. By strengthening Eastern Turkestan's autonomy in certain matters, Sheng was thereby leading it further and further away from genuine independence—and particularly from secession from China, which was the prime demand of the more resolutely inclined national leaders of the country.

The other side of the coin was that progress toward a certain measure of independence from China had a price and that price was growing economic, financial, political, and military dependence upon the Soviet Union.

How justified then is such a maneuver? And to what extent is an independence achieved at the price of a new dependence?

Many years were to pass before the Communist government of China finally succeeded in eliminating the results of the economic legacy left by Sheng. This occurred only after 1954, when, following the visit of Khrushchev and Bulganin to Peking, the Soviet-Chinese joint companies were abolished. The positions gained by the Soviets in Eastern Turkestan with so much trouble through intricate political stratagems were all lost. And lost in exchange for the polite phraseology of the Sino-Soviet communiqué which for the umpteenth time declared the firm and unbreakable friendship of the Soviet and Chinese peoples.

The American scholar W.A. Douglas Jackson commented: "The surrender was unprecedented in Russian history, not only did they give up an area in which they had long had a vital interest but they did so voluntarily. But it was a surrender, not to Nationalist China, to Japan, or to any other capitalistic country; it was a surrender to Communist China, to comrades in the international struggle."

It is easy to understand and evaluate the assessment of Sheng Shih-tsai that appeared in the Soviet press after many years of absolute silence: "Sheng Shih-tsai pursued a policy of the physical extermination of Communists and progressive elements from among the national minorities, which was linked with the 'anticommunist campaign' of Chiang Kai-shek in 1939-1943."

This belated political epitaph can hardly do justice to Sheng Shih-tsai. But then probably no epitaph ever does the subject justice, in the sense that one cannot describe in a few brief lines an entire human life with all its ups and downs. For this reason the above assessment can be neither an analysis, nor a summing up, nor an indictment of all that Sheng Shih-tsai did for Eastern Turkestan, for its liberation of colonial dependence, and for its continued existence as a part of China.

## Toward an Independent State of Turkestan

If one can speak of objective criteria attesting to the right of a people to independent statehood, such criteria must surely include a clearly defined national identity, a common history of sufficiently long standing, a tradition of statehood, and last but by no means least, the desire of the people themselves for such independent statehood. If we now try to apply all these criteria to Eastern Turkestan, we will find that they are very much in evidence, including a strong desire of the people for independent statehood.

The concept of an independent Eastern Turkestan state has passed through several stages in its history. The first stage relates to the period prior to its conquest and colonization by China. An Uighur state existed as far back as the eighth century. In 1001 an Uighur ambassador who was received in China with great honor told the emperor and his court that his country extended as far as the Hwang Ho in the east, and as far as the Snow Mountains in the west. In all probability the Uighur state ruled over many other vassal territories. The ambassador mentioned several hundred such small possessions.

The Uighur state obviously played a far from insignificant role in Eastern affairs in those years. Evidence of this is to be found in numerous references to the Uighurs in Arabian and Persian sources of the ninth-eleventh centuries. The Uighurs are also frequently mentioned in Chinese chronicles of that period. It is an interesting fact that, according to various sources, when the Chinese or Mongol emperors were in need of money, it was the Uighur rulers who acted as their creditors.

As Mahmud Ibn Hussein of Kashgar wrote, "They have an enormous city called Besh-Balyk which consists of five small towns and recently they have built the town of Yangi, which means 'New.' Towns like Tubut, Kingut, Kuzho, Kaami, Talas, and Turum are all Uighur frontier towns." So the Uighur state was characterized by a fairly high level of urbanization.

Their cultural development was fully in keeping with their level of state organization. Referring to them as "Turkestanians," one Chinese author has written about them with obvious deference: "The Turkestanians have various books: botanical, medical, fortune-telling, religious, historical, and chronicles and descriptions of different states. They teach that the sky is high and covers the earth, that the land is thick and maintains us, that the sun and the moon give us light, and therefore all these things must be worshipped. They forbid extortion, lechery, injustice, and lies; and they approve of circumspection and kind-heartedness."

This first phase of the Uighur state's existence lasted for something like 500 years.

The second phase marks the territory's transition to the status of a Chinese colony. But despite Chinese efforts to destroy the very idea of independent statehood, the state in Eastern Turkestan repeatedly rose, phoenixlike, from the ashes. If the reference to phoenix is purely allegorical, the ashes were very real. They were the ashes and smoking ruins left behind by the Chinese troops who overran the country again and again in their determination to return it to China.

Every time an insurrection seemed near to success, the attributes of independent government would promptly appear in Eastern Turkestan. As in any colonial war, the life of such independent governments was cut short by the blows of the Chinese expeditionary forces. Such was the fate of the Dunganian and Taranchin sultanates and of the other states and kingdoms.

One of the most successful and lasting attempts to restore Eastern Turkestan's statehood relates to the 1860s. For a full sixteen years the country existed apart from China. The upshot of that insurrection was the formation of two states: the Ili Sultanate in the northern part of Eastern Turkestan and the Kashgar Emirate headed by Yakub-bek in the south.

While China was vainly attempting to rob these states of their newly acquired independence by sending in a succession of armies, two other powers, Britain and Russia, began to display a heightened interest in them. In 1868 Yakub-bek received Captain Reintahl, a secret emissary of Britain. The cloak of secrecy was soon lifted, however, and there followed a series of official state visits: a Russian mission under Baron Kaulbas in 1872, a British mission headed by Forsyte in 1873 and 1874, a second visit by Captain Reintahl in 1875, and a Russian mission under Captain Kuropatkin in 1877.

All these foreign inroads would obviously have been out of the question if the rebellious state had not demonstrated its stability in the face of the Chinese colossus.

Russia was certainly following the developments in Eastern Turkestan very closely. Some leading Russian orientologists tended to regard the "independent Moslem state in China" as something that had come to stay. Even modern Chinese historians admit that the entire territory of Eastern Turkestan could easily have been lost to China forever as a result of these developments.

Once again the newly emergent states of Eastern Turkestan were finally crushed by the Chinese; but not so the yearning of the people for independent statehood. There probably exist some social laws—so far unknown and perhaps unknowable—which govern the birth and death of states. Perhaps they are a combination of economic, historical, ethnical, and other factors. Or they could be very different—somewhere outside all those factors. For it is all too frequently impossible to explain why a state that seems to have all it needs to exist indefinitely actually proves totally lacking in vitality. And, vice versa, it can be equally hard to explain the indestructibility of the rudiments of statehood in other cases, such as Eastern Turkestan.

As Yakub-bek's emirate lay in smoking ruins Russia was already anticipating new events and a reemergence of the states that had been destroyed so many times before.

"The political situation," wrote the Russian scholar P.P. Semyonov, "in our neighbouring territory cannot fail to concern the administration of Western Siberia. Today or tomorrow the country may regain its independence, and then easily fall under the influence of a powerful neighbour. Why should that neighbour be the British from India?"

These words proved truly prophetic in the sense that very soon this territory was troubled by uprisings which inevitably developed into anticolonial war and a struggle for independence. But this time it was not until the 1930s that the insurrection resulted in the emergence of yet another independent state.

A new Moslem republic of Eastern Turkestan was proclaimed in 1933 at Kashgar. Its government, headed by Sabit-Damla, declared the republic's complete secession from China. Fully alive to the importance of symbols of state in such situations, the government of Eastern Turkestan was prompt to introduce its own national flag designed in true Islamic fashion: the star and crescent on a white background.

Attempts by the republic of Eastern Turkestan to assert itself in the international arena were aimed primarily at India and Afghanistan. But Sabit-Damla's government did not have time to establish diplomatic relations with them. In 1934 a Chinese expeditionary force overran the territory of the republic which, after no more than two years of independence, was again turned into a Chinese colony.

As in the 1860s, Eastern Turkestan had been very close to achieving lasting independence. It would probably be safe to say that had the republic of Eastern Turkestan managed to hold out just a little longer, it would have been very difficult indeed for the Chinese to destroy it.

The events of those years, one Soviet scholar has written, "could have taken on such a scale that the Chinese government would have been faced with the danger of losing a province." Such an assessment is shared by Western scholars. According to one of them, the events in Eastern Turkestan at that time "nearly succeeded in breaking away the territory from China."

But the phoenix was indeed indestructible. Ten years later it was again destined to arise out of ashes—this time in the shape of the "Revolutionary Republic of Eastern Turkestan." As before, its chief slogans were independence and complete secession from China.

On January 5, 1945, the provisional government of the republic appealed to the peoples of Eastern Turkestan to rise against the Kuomintang. Since at that time the Kuomintang epitomized the dominant political and state power of China, the appeal meant in effect a declaration of war on China.

Underlying this challenge hurled in the face of the colonizing power was something more than simply another national or political doctrine. This time the challenge was backed by real military strength united under a single command. The republic's regular army had, according to various sources, a strength of somewhere between 10,000 and 40,000 men.

As such, these figures were not really very impressive. There were two factors, however, which lent them far greater weight than appears at first glance. The first was the general scale of the liberation movement in Eastern Turkestan. The second was the fact that the central Chinese government was exhausted by the struggle with the Communist armies that were besieging the bastions of its already waning power. Bound hand and foot by the civil war, the central government was compelled to accept the confrontation.

China had no alternative but to start negotiations with the Revolutionary Republic of Eastern Turkestan. They lasted for a full eight months, and the treaty signed as a result of the talks was an attempt to reconcile the irreconcilable: the desire of Eastern Turkestan for independence and China's determination to thwart it.

The leaders of the republic believed the treaty could save it from being crushed by China's military strength—a fate that had overcome so many of its predecessors. The price for such guarantees proved sufficiently high, however—so high in fact as to exceed the value of the newly won freedom. The republic had to give up the slogan of secession from China and be content with autonomy within China. In the words of one former leader of the Revolutionary Republic of Eastern Turkestan, "At the beginning we proclaimed in Ili an Eastern Turkestan republic—another separatist successor, that is, to the republic of Kashgar of ten years earlier, but after the peace treaty with the Kuomintang of June 1946 we dropped that title and we buried our separatism."

For both parties the treaty was obviously no more than a maneuver, and they were both fully aware of this. It was quite plain that whoever mustered enough strength to violate it would be the victor. If China could have done so this would have meant the complete and unconditional suppression of all separatist tendencies in Eastern Turkestan and its incorporation in China. If the republic's leaders could have been the first to tip the scales in their favor, they would have done so to achieve final and lasting secession from China.

"It may have seemed, then," one Western observer has written, "that Sinkiang would follow the same road Outer Mongolia took and become, under Soviet guidence, a republic on Soviet lines."

The attitude of the Chinese government of the time to Eastern Turkestan may be summed up as follows: "In view of its strategic location in the heartland of Asia it could contribute toward the peace and security of Asia and of the world only if it remained under the complete sovereignty of the Republic of China."

Those words belong to Chiang Kai-shek. But they could just as well have been uttered by Mao Tse-tung. For, as subsequent events were to show, in this matter the Kuomintang and its sworn enemies, the Communists, were of one mind. This is only too natural. Once in power, either of those political forces inevitably became an instrument of the state. And the state promptly began dictating the line of behavior that was optimal from the standpoint of the functioning of the state as a system. One of the prerequisites of the optimalization of a system is preservation of its integrity. This is the explanation behind the identical policies pursued by different successive Chinese governments in respect of the national minorities—from the Ching emperor to the Kuomintang and from the Kuomintang to the great Mao and his present successors.

Throughout 1947–1949 thousands of people in Turkestan were subjected to reprisals and executed on charges of seeking "to detach Sinkiang from China." Referring to the years of confrontation between the Kuomintang and the national liberation forces of Eastern Turkestan, *Jenmin Juhpao* (the *People's Daily*) names a figure of 12,000 people massacred in prisons and concentration camps. This figure may well be true. All the more significant was the number of victims later, when the policy of the "inalienability of Sinkiang from China" began to be pursued by the Communist party cadres sent into the country from Peking.

In 1948 a vast group of Kazakhs, unable to stand the terror any longer, decided to abandon their homes and leave Eastern Turkestan. But in defiance of traditional Russian policy, Stalin refused to accept them and the Soviet frontier was slammed shut in their faces. Twenty thousand families with their children and their herds then turned to the south. They moved across an arid desert and made their way slowly through the snow-clad mountain passes of Tibet. This mass exodus went on for two years. Thousands of graves marked their route. Only one out of every four of the original travelers reached Kashmir. From there the survivors were sent on to Turkey.

The question of secession was formally withdrawn from the political agenda after the formation in Eastern Turkestan of a pro-Communist government in September 1949. This government promptly declared that the province was joining the so-called "liberated" areas of China.

But the drive for independence could not be arrested by this purely formal act. Anti-Chinese trends continued even after 1949. "As a result," one Chinese author noted, "several dozens of honest Chinese suffered."

True enough, with incorporation in the Chinese People's Republic, the campaign of terror that had been conducted in the area by Kuomintang Chinese ended—but only to be replaced with a still more monstrous campaign of terror, this time instigated by other Chinese, calling themselves Communists.

Like the Burmese peasant who harvests two crops a year, the Chinese reaped a double crop of heads in Eastern Turkestan. First came the Kuomintang, then the Maoists. Anyone who could be associated with the idea of secession from China was physically eliminated.

As before, the reprisals were of a plainly colonialist type. And as before, Han Chinese took the part of hatchet-men, their victims being local national leaders.

Once in Eastern Turkestan, the Chinese Communist forces crushed the major military–political groupings under local leaders such as Osman, Iulbars, and Urazbai. Their fate was shared soon afterwards by Samud Sabri, Iolbas, and other prominent local figures.

But the task of beheading the nationalist movement would have fallen short of fulfillment if Peking had not succeeded at the same time in doing away with another group of Turkestan leaders, namely its own followers. The politically naïve may regard it as an appalling thing for a regime to destroy its own allies. But this should cause no surprise to those who are familiar, if not with the ruthless laws of the game of politics, then at least with the rules of the game of chess. In it the players frequently have to sacrifice one of their own men for the sake of gaining a superior position or simply to escape a dangerous situation.

The popularity and prestige of the pro-Communist leaders among the local people were too great not to pose any potential threat to Peking's leadership. This was all the more true since the Communist leaders of Eastern Turkestan themselves were loath to give up their dream of an independent Turkestan. They insisted, for instance, on having their own Communist party of China and they demanded the retention of such attributes of independence as their own coat of arms and national flag. This stand taken by the local leaders proved in effect, however, to be yet one more nail in their coffin. The only question was how these last remaining Eastern Turkestan leaders could be removed. It was merely a question of choosing the right method.

The method the Chinese Communists finally chose was by then becoming almost traditional. Some time previously Manchuria had been ruled by Chang Tso-lin, with Japanese backing. No sooner did he acquire too great a political weight and prestige in his country than the Japanese, fearing for their position in Manchuria, decided it was time to remove him. As always the Japanese secret service acted swiftly and surely. A train crash eliminated Chang Tso-lin from the path of the Japanese.

Another similar fact relates to the World War II period. There was at that time a well-known Indian nationalist leader, Subhas Chandra Bhose, who also enjoyed Japanese backing. No sooner did he gain too great a popularity among his compatriots than the Japanese began seeking a way to get rid of him. Like Chang Tso-lin, Subhas Chandra Bhose died in an accident. The plane carrying him to Tokyo happened to crash.

Now as the four last remaining political leaders of Eastern Turkestan were boarding a plane that was to take them to Peking, there were probably some Chinese among those who had come to see them off who knew that the plane would never reach Peking. The plane crash was followed by obviously prearranged funeral rites with formal condolences from Peking and all the other trimmings.

The advantages of this method of beheading a political movement are obvious. First and foremost because it provokes the least possible negative public repercussions in comparison with a phony trial on trumped up political charges. And this was particularly important in Eastern Turkestan in those postwar years.

It is interesting to note that the politicians summarily dealt with as a result of these "accidents" and "disasters" maintained their loyalty to their murderers, whether Japanese or Chinese, until their dying breath. But there was no loyalty that could save them from the fate in store for them. For those who engineered their removal it was simply a matter of political necessity.

As subsequent events were to prove, however, even this double-edged attack on the exponents of independence proved incapable of destroying the drive for independence in Eastern Turkestan. (This, incidentally, provides added proof that the destruction of the exponents of an idea can never be a reliable method of destroying the idea itself.)

The formation in Eastern Turkestan of local organs of self-government was a convenient form of earmarking candidates for the next wave of reprisals. True enough, as soon as the next batch of national cadres had been elevated to positions of authority, they were promptly and effectively done away with. Characteristically, the accusation leveled at them was no different from the one invoked by the Kuomintang in carrying out similar operations. The charge was nationalism or an attempt to detach Sinkiang from China.

The signal for the massacre of the national elite was sounded by the plenary meeting of the Chinese Communist Party Committee of the Sinkiang–Uighur Autonomous Region, which ended on April 30, 1958. At the meeting special party emissaries from Peking had accused the local cadres of demanding that the national question be resolved in China according to the Soviet pattern and of advocating among other things the equality of national cadres with Chinese. The reprisals began immediately after the meeting had been adjourned. Among the victims were the head of the Ili county, Abduraim Isa; the mayor of Urumchi, Abduraim Saidi; the chief of the department of internal affairs of the Sinkiang–Uighur Autonomous Region, Ibrahim Turdy; and the chief of the culture department, Ziya Samidi. Earlier the leader of the Kazakh community residing in Eastern Turkestan, Osman Bator, had likewise been executed. Other victims of the purge were Burhan Shahidi, a former chairman of the People's Government of Sinkiang and vice-chairman of the People's Political Consultative Council of the Chinese People's Republic, and Iminov, one of the leaders of the National Liberation Movement in Eastern Turkestan. Even this brief list of names and official titles provides some indication of the rank and national identity of those subjected to reprisals.

As so often happens—it was primarily the intelligentsia that appeared as the exponent of national consciousness. No wonder therefore that the intelligentsia was the prime target of this punitive operation. As the secretary of the Sinkiang–Uighur Committee of the Chinese Communist party, Saifuddin, emphasized, local nationalism had "become the most dangerous ideological trend," particularly among the intelligentsia. Reiterating the Communist position, Saifuddin pointedly stressed the inalienability of Eastern Turkestan from China.

The arrests, executions, and concentration camps did not only affect the living. Even the dead came in for their share of castigation.

Among them was the well-known Uighur poet, Lutfulla Mutalip, who had been killed in 1945 by the Kuomintang. Some time previously his family had been presented with a special diploma bearing Mao's signature and listing Mutalip's great services to the revolution. Having first been posthumously proclaimed a national hero, he was now, also posthumously, declared a nationalist and a pan-Turkoman.

The total number of purge victims defies even approximate calculation. Various figures have been named. One of them has been cited by the Chairman of the National Committee for the Liberation of Eastern Turkestan, U. Alptekin. According to his statement, reported by the Austrian Press agency on December 18, 1969, about 300,000 of the local population had been massacred since Chinese troops entered Eastern Turkestan in 1949.

The scale of the punitive operations carried out by Chinese forces can be assessed by the fact that between 1950 and 1954 alone 880 regular Chinese army units had taken part in action against the "bandits." This terrifying human meat grinder is still working to this day.

According to the stories told by refugees, enlarged photographs of the victims of executions or reprisals are displayed prominently from time to time at Urumchi and other towns of Eastern Turkestan. Photographs through which a red line has been painted stand for "shot." In most cases this mark is to be seen on photographs of young people.

Some of them are mere children of twelve or thirteen. The old people (many refugees have mentioned the names of seventy- and seventy-five-year-old Uighurs) are usually sentenced to fifteen years imprisonment—which in effect is the same as if they had been sentenced to death.

For weeks on end the fading photos of the victims hang in the streets, frightening the passersby. This method of intimidation goes back to the medieval custom of displaying the heads of executed criminals on a spear or hanging them inside a cage as was done in China even within living memory.

This combination of the medieval in content and the modern in method (it is after all only photographs that are displayed and not the actual heads) is a feature that is highly characteristic of present-day China and is manifested in a variety of forms.

On the whole, however, events in Eastern Turkestan are shrouded in secrecy. "It seems impossible," wrote the Swedish explorer Sven Hedin a little earlier, "to obtain any reliable information about events in Sinkiang from places outside the frontiers of the province. Not even in China is anything definite known about what is happening there."

To a certain extent those words explain why information about Eastern Turkestan relating to the period of the Cultural Revolution is so fragmentary and incomplete. The mass unrest in the area ostensibly assumed the form of protests against the numerous campaigns carried out by Peking. In fact, however, these protests had a far deeper and more meaningful undercurrent. As always, they were primarily motivated by demands for the secession of Eastern Turkestan from China and for independent statehood. The scale of these protests may be assessed even through the meager information emanating from China. Some big-character posters appearing at the height of the Cultural Revolution in Peking, for instance, made mention of 10,000 "reactionaries" who had rebelled in one of the towns of Eastern Turkestan. "Some of the commanders," the poster complained, "had laid down their weapons as they faced the masses." In the town of Urumchi alone, over 100,000 people had taken part in anti-Chinese protests, according to the Red Guard press. In many cases these protests seem to have been quite well organized. Stanley Karnow mentions in this connection some armed groups who hid in the

mountains and operated a radio station named "Voice of the Guer-
rillas."

It is significant that even in this atmosphere of outright military
terror the various nationalities of Eastern Turkestan did not give up
their attempts to regain their national independence. One such attempt was made in 1958, when the Kazakhs tried to declare an
independent Kazakh Republic with Kuldja as its center. This attempt,
like many others of its kind, was ruthlessly stamped out by the
Chinese troops.

In all probability, the concept of an independent Eastern Turkestan
is beginning to find support not only among the local nationalities.
Numerous resettlers from China are beginning to associate themselves
less and less with the remote central regions of China proper. According to many Uighur refugees now in Russia, quite a few Han Chinese,
particularly those living in the area for a long time, have frequently
supported the efforts aimed at separating Eastern Turkestan from
China. In other words, the situation is becoming very similar to what
once happened in Manchuria.


## Blood Brothers and Faith Brothers

In the world today there is probably no other religious community
that can match the Moslem world, extending as it does from the
Pacific to the Atlantic. The world of Islam, which unites on the basis
of one faith people of diverse nationality, historical traditions, and
territory, has always displayed the greatest solidarity toward its members, the solidarity of coreligionists. There was a time when this
solidarity also extended to the Moslems living in Chinese colonial
bondage. These Moslems consist of two basic ethnic groups. They are
either Turkomans (Uighurs, Kazakhs, and Kirghiz) or Chinese proper,
whose forefathers embraced Islam (Hui or Dunganians). Regardless,
however, of these national or ethnic distinctions, from the very beginning of the Chinese conquest the peoples of Eastern Turkestan stood
together as one community united by a common religion. "Be
Moslems!" was the battle cry of the leaders of anti-Chinese uprisings.
In later times the slogan of a holy war, the "Gazavat," was more than

once the banner rallying different national groups in Eastern Turkestan.

It goes to the credit of the Moslems of Central Asia that they never forget or forsake their brothers in faith locked inside the hostile land of the Chinese state. When the Moslems living in China raised insurrections in the first half of the last century crowds of volunteers would stream to their assistance from Central Asia. Following their religious leaders they joined the fight in thousands. In some cases these voluntary forces were even formed in the territory of Central Asia. Such was the allied army of Mohammed Yusuf-hoja, made up of people from Kokand, Tashkent, Tajikistan, and refugees from Eastern Turkestan. In 1830, coming to the aid of the insurgents, this army expelled the Chinese from a sizable portion of Eastern Turkestan. Instances of this kind of voluntary aid to the Moslems in Eastern Turkestan from Central Asia were registered in later periods as well. This Moslem solidarity, however, was a two-edged weapon when it became known in Eastern Turkestan that czarist troops were committing injustices in Central Asia. There were, for instance, demonstrations by local citizens outside the czarist consulate at Kuldja. These facts of the mutual and bilateral solidarity of Moslems prove more convincingly than many other arguments that the forcible division of Turkestan is a completely abnormal phenomenon.

The later uprisings of the 1850s and 1860s in Eastern Turkestan were also actively assisted by volunteers from Central Asia. For it was to them, their brothers in faith, that the insurgents always appealed for aid. And they received aid, including material support through organized collections.

The Chinese colonial authorities knew quite enough about all these goings on to realize that they could never hope to achieve their goals without first severing these ties. This could be attained only in one way: by bringing under control the source from which the Eastern Turkestan Moslems received aid and support. A boa constrictor cannot digest a whole rabbit by only half swallowing him. But that is exactly what had happened with Turkestan. So, immediately conquering Eastern Turkestan, China began preparing to swallow its other half. Rumors about the impending conquest "alarmed the entire Moslem world." The local Central Asian beys pooled their military efforts, while the powerful Kandahar ruler, Ahmed-Shah, sent out a special detachment to help defend Tashkent from the Chinese. This solidarity of the Moslem world forced the Chinese emperor to abandon his plans for a Central Asian campaign.

The traditional solidarity of Central Asia with Eastern Turkestan survives to this day. When the scale of reprisals and executions became unbearable, the people of Eastern Turkestan began to look across the border for salvation, as they had done so many times before. It was particularly easy to escape until 1954 as the frontier between Soviet Russia and Eastern Turkestan was in effect open and the local population could go back and forth without any formalities. But when, in the 1960s, many inhabitants of Eastern Turkestan applied to the Chinese authorities for exit visas to travel to Russia, the only response they got was machine-gun fire. A crowd of Kazakhs was machine-gunned point blank at Ili. In May 1962 a throng of 2000 was fired at in Kuldja; two hundred of them were mown down. They had been demanding permission to join their relatives in Soviet Central Asia. Quoting Hong Kong refugee sources, *The Times* of London wrote that "troops fired on demonstrators, killing a number of them."

In the spring of 1962 there was a sudden rush toward the border. Carrying their children and their miserably wretched possessions and driving their cattle before them, they fled as if escaping from fire or an enemy invasion. In the course of a few days 60,000 people crossed the border into the territory of Central Asia.

The repercussions of this event were far too loud for Peking to ignore. And it went too far against the usual Chinese propaganda stories about religious tolerance and the national paradise that allegedly existed in China. The statement made by Chou En-lai about this incident was far from convincing: "In 1962 under the instigation and direct command of forces from abroad, a group of the most reactionary protagonists of local nationalism staged a traitorous counterrevolutionary armed rebellion in Ining (Kuldja), Sinkiang, and assisted and organized the flight abroad of a large number of people near the frontier."

The first wave of refugees was followed by others. The Soviet consulates were besieged by people who wanted to leave Eastern Turkestan. At the demand of the Chinese authorities, all Soviet consulates in the province were closed down. But this belated measure did little to solve the problem. The flight across the Soviet border continued. Between 1959 and 1966 100,000 Uighurs crossed into Central Asia.

Some of the refugees have related that in recent years a non-Han Chinese was practically unable to find a job in Eastern Turkestan. On the Soviet side they found not only employment but also plenty of opportunities to learn a trade.

The Uighurs remaining in Eastern Turkestan are making a desperate effort to save what remains of their culture from being completely sinified. On the Russian side they have several newspapers printed in their own language, using the traditional Arabic script. Among other things, there is an Uighur Theater of Music and Drama at Alma-Ata and a folk song and dance company at Tashkent.

There would thus seem to be no reason for not feeling themselves quite at home in the country that has given them asylum. However, having permitted the refugees from Eastern Turkestan to settle in Central Asia, the Soviet authorities found they now had a problem on their hands. Many thousands of young Uighurs, Kirghiz, and Kazakhs who had been forced to flee are rearing to go back to China to take part in the armed struggle against the Chinese. It has required a considerable effort on the part of the Soviet authorities to restrain them from undesirable excesses.

"So you want to fight for independence," the authorities tell the more impatient of the refugees. "That is your right. But just consider the kind of enemy you will have to deal with. Would it not be better to study the art of war first?"

This certainly sounds reasonable and convincing. But the long-drawn-out training involving all sorts of military colleges, schools, and courses which the former subjects of China are attending has another side to it. Though Freud is not generally recognized in the Soviet Union, this method is plainly one of those things that Freud would have called sublimation. The military training which has been dragging on for many years now may be regarded as a kind of safety device used by the Soviet authorities to draw off the excess energy of the most extremist-minded refugees. In other words, the protracted military training may be seen as a form of restraint.

How much longer will the Russians be able to hold these forces in check? For when, sooner or later, they break loose, the outcome will amount to much more than simply the beginning of an insurrection in Eastern Turkestan.

As I mentioned earlier, the armies that came to the aid of insurgencies in Eastern Turkestan in the past were recruited from among volunteers in Central Asia. If events of this kind were to break out in Turkestan tomorrow, the tacit appeal for solidarity would be answered by hundreds of thousands of Kazakhs, Kirghiz, and Uzbeks in Central Asia. This readiness to come to the aid of brothers in blood and in faith is nowhere stronger than among the Asian peoples. Suffice it to recall the example of Vietnam where the northerners are helping the southerners. That is why, if the Soviet authorities should ever try to prevent the Central Asian volunteers from coming to the aid of their kinsmen their efforts may well be of no avail.

For the time being, however, the prospective rebels from Eastern Turkestan are continuing to learn all there is to know about various types of arms, the art of war, and methods of guerrilla warfare. The *Far Eastern Economic Review*, which has reported this military training, has put the strength of this "army in emigration" at 60,000 men.

Is that a large number or not? The answer will be found by analysis of some well-known precedents. Thus, the noted military theoretician, F.O. Mikshe, has pointed out that in Algeria 20,000 rebels forced an occupation army 400,000-strong into inaction and virtual surrender. Several military authorities believe it is quite enough for a mere 2 percent of the population to participate in a guerrilla war for a mass regular army to be powerless to bring the situation under control.

According to the ratio mentioned by Mikshe, an army of 60,000 should be quite enough to tie down in Eastern Turkestan as many as 1.5 million Chinese troops. If we add to those 60,000 the hundreds of thousands of insurgents who are usually carried away by the wave of an uprising, it will be easy to imagine the scale of the new Vietnam that China is very likely to get into.

The prospect of Eastern Turkestan becoming a new Vietnam is far more real than may appear at first glance. Realizing how dangerous are the ties linking the Moslems of China with the world of Islam, Chinese imperial policy has always been to extend the limits of Chinese colonial possessions by including Central Asia in their number. But the unity and solidarity of the Moslems have always been successful in foiling those plans.

The Chinese then began thinking along different lines. Since the main link connecting the people of Turkestan with the outside world was Islam, the best way out would be to break that link, that is, to destroy Islam. With this in mind, Tso Tsun-tang, a governor general of the territory in the last century, ordered the closing of all Moslem schools, the banning of Moslem customs and rights, and the compulsory learning of Chinese.

In the Chinese Empire the persecution of Moslems was accompanied by various behavioral restrictions that were specially meant to humiliate Moslems.

"Upon encountering a Chinese official," wrote the Russian traveler Kuropatkin, "in the street, all Moslems were supposed to dismount. If the local *amban* was making a tour of the town, the people were supposed to kneel in the streets. If the amban was on his way to the temple, all Moslems, including the hakimbek, were supposed to kneel at the entrance with their hands behind their backs."

Another Russian traveler, Grum-Grzhimailo, who also visited Eastern Turkestan noted that the Chinese used to force the officials of the native administration to go to Chinese temples. This occurs, he explained, "wherever such violence could not meet with any real resistance."

Officials of the Chinese colonial administration probably had some grounds for equating loyalty to Islam with loyalty to a world beyond the limits of the Celestial Empire. This contained a potential tendency toward breaking away from Peking's orbit. In this sense loyalty to Islam was inherently antagonistic to the concept of China's unity and indivisibility. This was why Tso Tsun-tang tried to carry out one of the main purges in Eastern Turkestan according to the principle of religious affiliation. In one of his reports to the emperor he requested permission to kill not only armed Moslems, but also all Moslems, including children. "Whether he received that permission or not remains unknown," writes the Russian scholar M. Viukov, "but it was quite possible that this cruel measure was indeed taken." All this served to identify the term Moslem with a separatist aiming to break the territory away from China. In this, as in so many other questions of colonial policy and practice, there is a complete continuity between the imperial government, the Kuomintang, and the Chinese Communists. Like the colonial administration that preceded it, the Chinese Communist party accuses the Moslems of "regionalism," which in the parlance of present-day China is synonymous with "separatism." The ideological basis of this tendency toward separatism is solidarity with coreligionists outside China, loyalty to the Islamic tenet which proclaims all Moslems to be brothers.

The present rulers of China have, however, gone much further in suppressing Islam than the imperial officials or the Kuomintang ever did.

In 1958 countless numbers of Moslem clergy were brought to trial in Eastern Turkestan. The servants of Islam were charged with having "deceived and oppressed the people for many years," as the Chinese press reported. In 1959 the Chinese authorities forced 4000 imams and mullahs to suspend their religious duties, discard their traditional dress, and engage in physical labor. Instead of poring over their sacred texts, the students of the Koran and the religious leaders and teachers of the faith had to arm themselves with picks and shovels and dedicate themselves to cleaning out irrigation ditches and sweeping the streets.

Li Ming, a Chinese who escaped from China and now lives in the town of Ussuriisk, described the most elaborate indignities to which Moslems are subjected in China. For instance they are forced to keep pigs and eat pork.

But the main blow against Islam as a form of the public consciousness was struck during the Cultural Revolution. Humiliations and mockery of the religious feelings of Moslems assumed a mass scale. This Peking-inspired campaign was accompanied by an appalling desecration of sacred shrines and the destruction and ravaging of mosques. The local people were powerless to resist this wave of pogroms carried out by Chinese, most of whom had come from elsewhere in the country. The desecration and closure of all the eight mosques in Urumchi, for instance, was carried out by Red Guards who had specially traveled all the way from Peking.

Some reports about these events did reach the outside world at the time. However, except for a few purely token protests, the Moslem world remained strangely indifferent to the reports. The governments of Moslem nations did not react at all to this mass religious terror or to the devastation and desecration of mosques in Eastern Turkestan— surely a glaring contrast with their reaction to the attempt to set fire to the mosque in Jerusalem. Could this have been because that particular episode concerned an Arab mosque? If that is so, then surely the national feelings have prevailed over the unity of faith in the Moslem world? In that case, the Moslem world exists no more in the lofty ethical sense in which it used to exist. A community that so easily betrays its own children thereby dooms itself to inevitable death.

The fact that the people of Eastern Turkestan were forsaken in their most critical hour by the Moslem world has had irreversible consequences for Islam. For all that the Chinese emperors, the Kuomintang, and even Mao had proved powerless to accomplish happened. Of situations such as this the ancient Indian laws of Manu say: "My enemy threw a stone at me. But I laughed. My friend struck me with a flower, and I was hurt." When the enemy tried to suppress Islam in Eastern Turkestan, Islam stood it all, staunch and invincible. But when the friend, the Moslem world beyond the borders of Turkestan, turned away and betrayed it, something in the soul of the people broke, died, never to revive. As soon as the basic ethical law of Islam—that all Moslems are brothers—was abandoned and relegated to oblivion, the fate of Islam in China was sealed.

In the meantime, recent history bears witness to a totally different state of affairs. In the last century several Russian sinologists predicted that the whole of China would some day be converted to Islam. At that time such a trend was definitely in evidence. For the non-Moslem peoples Islam then had a powerful appeal. But when the basic principle of Islam, the solidarity of all Moslems, was betrayed, that appeal dimmed. What was once a creed vigorously endeavoring to extend its frontiers now became an ideology seeking only to stay within the existing ones. But the example of Eastern Turkestan proves that even in this it has not always been successful.

So the fact that the brothers in faith found themselves forsaken in time of trouble only partially affected Eastern Turkestan. The harm it did to Islam itself was a thousand times worse. There are figures to prove this. In old China, Moslems numbered 50 million. According to figures made public in Peking after the Communist takeover, the figure dropped to 35 million. And some time ago a new figure of 10 million was mentioned. No one can today say for certain how low the figure has dropped after the events of the Cultural Revolution.

Whether or not Islam will manage to keep its head above water in this world of competing ideologies depends on the conclusions that are drawn from the past by the leaders of the Moslem world. Will they succeed in returning to the former policy of Moslem solidarity and in reviewing their attitude to Eastern Turkestan? Or will they allow regional and national interests finally to prevail over the common cause of all Moslems and thereby obliterate that cause?

In this context Eastern Turkestan is the arena where not only the future of that territory but also the future of Islam itself is being decided.

## On the Threshold of Extinction

The early Spanish explorers used to exchange trinkets, beads, and colored ribbons for Indian gold. The trinket in exchange for which the Chinese obtained Eastern Turkestan's renunciation of the slogan of independence was their promise of "local autonomy." In contrast to the European colonizers, the Chinese did not give their "natives" even a chance to play with the trinket. Peking was just as swift in taking back the "local autonomy" as it had been in granting it.

In the first Joint People's Democratic Government of Eastern Turkestan 29 of the 31 members were representatives of the local minorities and only two were Chinese. This ratio was reasonable and fair. It reflected the proportion of Chinese among the total population, which was about 3 percent. After a short period of time, however, the ratio began to change. The proportion of Chinese in leading government and party bodies rose to 50 percent. Then it went still higher and reached 90 percent. In the secretariat of the former party committee of the Sinkiang-Uighur Autonomous Region, ten leading posts were filled by Chinese and only one by a representative of the local people. And finally, in the new revolutionary committee set up during the Cultural Revolution, all the ranking leaders are Chinese. The disappearance of the last representative of the local nationalities in the government of the province marked the disappearance of the last semblance of "autonomy." At present, only Chinese are represented on all the party, administrative, and economic bodies in Sinkiang.

Among the local population the swift sinification of the government could not fail to provoke a painful reaction. This reaction may be judged by the accusations made by the Maoist party functionaries against the local national forces. According to Saifuddin, for instance, those forces assert that all leading posts in the Eastern Turkestan party apparatus are held by Han people and they demand the ouster of the Chinese. There have also been other reports of demands that the Chinese officials should be expelled from the province together with the Chinese resettlers.

The demands of the nationalist forces have been formulated even more bluntly by Liu Ko-ping, at one time chairman of the Nationalities Affairs Committee: "This (Sinkiang) will be a genuinely autonomous region only if the Han cadres are gone. So long as they remain here there will be no real autonomy. So long as Han cadres remain (in autonomous areas) the national minorities will not be able to exercise their power. All Han cadres should be evacuated from national minorities' areas."

It would be naïve to expect that the Peking leaders would comply with these demands. The removal of the Chinese administration and its replacement by national personnel could lead finally to the breaking away of this province from China. Naturally neither Mao himself nor his successors could agree to this. True enough, for appearance's sake an Uighur to start with still remained at the head of the province; Saifuddin so suited the central government that he was probably the only provincial leader not to suffer during the Cultural Revolution. His hour, however, has also come. In January 1978 Saifuddin was dismissed from his post and at last a Chinese, Wan Feng, was appointed in his place.

But the imposition of leading Chinese cadres is but one part of the assimilation program carried through by Peking. Having undermined the foundations of the common religious consciousness of the Eastern Turkestan people, Peking's colonial experts have paved the way for the next step, the total destruction of a common national consciousness.

Schopenhauer once suggested a method of resolving the Jewish question by making Jews stop identifying themselves as a single community. It would suffice to permit and encourage mixed marriages, he wrote, for the Jews to disappear in a hundred years. The present-day Chinese policymakers have come to the same conclusion: To destroy a national community it should be mixed, diluted, and dissolved in a bigger national community. But to reach that conclusion they had no need to read Schopenhauer. They had only to address themselves to past colonial practices of the Chinese Empire. During the T'ang dynasty (seventh–tenth centuries B.C.), when the lands of the Uighurs were conquered by the Chinese, about one million Uighurs were forcibly resettled deep inside the country. The purpose was to achieve the ethnic absorption of the alien national group by the Han.

What the Ching emperors failed to accomplish is being actively brought to a conclusion today. The task of destroying the Uighurs, begun more than one thousand years ago, is in good hands and the method being used is the same. The only difference is that instead of deporting Uighurs to China, Chinese immigrants are flooding Eastern Turkestan. The same thing has already happened in Manchuria with the same consequences. Only in Eastern Turkestan the pace is much faster.

It is worth emphasizing that the influx of young people, mainly men, is occurring in areas where reprisals, arrests, and exile have carried away a sizable part of the local male population. This process of substitution naturally could not fail to remain without demographical consequences. The number of mixed marriages rose sharply. But this was precisely what the Chinese authorities had in mind. There have been reports, for instance, that graduates of Nanking and Canton Universities gave written pledges to settle in Eastern Turkestan and marry Uighur girls. Refugees arriving from Eastern Turkestan have said that between 30 and 40 percent of all children now born in the area come from mixed marriages. Naturally enough, all these children are officially listed as Chinese.

The program calling for an extensive Chinese resettlement drive into the western regions was announced directly after the introduction of Chinese troops into Eastern Turkestan in March 1950. In 1959 a new program was announced calling for the transformation of Eastern Turkestan into a base for the production of steel, oil, and coal. Naturally enough, this program was advertised by official propaganda as yet another manifestation of the Chinese people's solicitude for the national borderlands. But beware the Greeks bearing gifts! The Trojan horse sent from Peking was chock full of Chinese immigrants. It was explained that the program could be carried into effect only through an enormous influx of outside labor. This was exactly what the sponsors of the program had in mind all along, knowing, as they did, about the low levels of technical equipment in China. Through this one step, Peking succeeded in attaining three objectives. The first was to intensify the development of the mineral resources of the territory. The second was to enhance the economic ties linking the territory with central China. And the third was to populate Eastern Turkestan with Chinese.

In 1950, when the immigration program was just beginning, the proportion of Chinese in Eastern Turkestan was no higher than 3 percent; by 1957 it had risen to 10 percent; in 1962 it was 20.5 percent; in 1964 it was almost 45 percent; in 1969 it had reached over 50 percent.

In 1977 I met Uighurs, refugees from Sinkiang. According to them the proportion of Chinese in the province's population continues to grow.

As a result, the indigenous nationalities—Uighurs, Kazakhs, Kirghiz—have already become national minorities in their own land.

But the Chinese have no intention of contenting themselves with what they have already achieved. As Alptekin declared in the statement quoted above, Peking has set itself the goal of resettling up to 70 million Chinese in the area. At the same time it is determined to reduce the Turki population drastically.

All this has in no way brought the area any closer to the state of pacification which Peking is so anxious to attain. "In one short sentence, the sinification of Sinkiang has progressed far enough to embitter the local population against the Chinese rulers, though not far enough to make Chinese rule appear secure," wrote Klaus Menert.

The traditional mistrust and wariness of the people of Turkestan toward all that emanates from Peking was noted even by an ancient Chinese author. "The people of Turkestan," he wrote, "are by nature distrustful and they do not trust all that you tell them." We now know that their mistrust was based on bitter experience. In recent years this experience has been confirmed time and time again. Unfortunately, it is rather doubtful whether the people of Turkestan will ever get a chance to profit by that experience.

In Eastern Turkestan today the policy of national assimilation has ceased to be secret policy. The absorption of local nationalities has been proclaimed an official target. This is indeed something that knows no precedent in history—as so much else in China, for that matter.

The Chinese press has bluntly stated that the aim of Peking's nationalities policy is "the complete elimination of national distinctions and differences."

One manifestation of such distinctions and differences is language. The elimination of national languages in Eastern Turkestan has, therefore, been declared by the Chinese one of the prime and urgent objectives of that policy. "Language," *Sinkiang Jihpao* (the *Sinkiang Daily*) has written, "must serve the unification of the motherland; in other words, the languages of the minority people must be made as close as possible to the language of Han people."

"We must not be oblivious of the fact," the paper went on to say, "that although the languages of the national minorities played an important part in their cultural development, they have become incompatible with the needs of the leap forward in economic construction and cultural revolution."

These words surely speak for themselves.

———

The events of recent years in Eastern Turkestan are in many ways irreversible. The sole chance its people still have to escape complete assimilation and national extinction lies in reconstituting themselves in an independent state, a state equally independent of both China and the Soviet Union.

Will the peoples of Eastern Turkestan take that chance? And will their blood brothers and brothers in faith come to their aid? All these are questions which for the time being must remain unanswered.

# PART II

# 5

# THEY WANT TO SECEDE

The patchwork structure of China is reflected even in its symbols of state. After 1911 when the Chinese revolutionary leaders decided that the new republic should have a suitable national flag of its own, their final choice was a banner with five stripes. These were supposed to symbolize the five different nationalities making up China: Han, Manchu, Mongols, Tibetans, and Moslems. In those years the Chinese Republic was referred to in official documents as "the republic of five nationalities." Subsequent Chinese leaders did their best to play down these symbols of China's divisibility. Chiang Kai-shek went out of his way to emphasize the concept of a single Chinese nation. But there was nothing in the world anyone could do to deny China's multinational composition or to diminish the urge of the non-Han Chinese to break away from China.

In the preceding chapters I described how Manchuria, Mongolia, Eastern Turkestan, and Tibet have for decades been constantly striving to secede and regain their independence. Their efforts have been treated with sympathy and understanding by China's neighbors—an attitude that is only too natural since they have but recently won their own freedom from colonial dependence. Commenting on the struggle of the non-Han peoples of China for their national liberation, the Indian periodical, *Link*, wrote: "Areas like Tibet and Sinkiang had an independent political existence and the semifeudal relations which they had with Peking when Chinese imperial power was at its zenith, does not make them part of China."

The urge to secede and form their own independent states is more or less uppermost in the minds of the lesser nationalities of China as well.

There are about 50 different non-Han peoples in China today. They are estimated to number between 42 and 43 million. Around 8 or 10 million are Chuang, 4 million Uighurs, 4 million Hui or Dunganians, 3.3 million Yi, 2.4 million Manchu, 1.5 million Mongols, etc. Though comprising only 6 percent of the total population of China, the national minorities occupy 50 to 60 percent of the land area, much of it rich in natural resources.

The desire of the lesser minorities to gain independence may be illustrated by the example of the Hui people. Like the other, larger nationalities, the Hui are also split in two by a provincial boundary. Like the inhabitants of other national areas, they want representatives of the indigenous nationality, and not Han Chinese, to be their administrative and party leaders. Like the Mongols, the Tibetans, and other non-Han peoples, they are making attempts to restore their statehood and set up "an independent Islamic kingdom."

These aspirations are all the more significant if we recall that the independence-seeking Hui people are in fact Chinese whose forefathers embraced the Islam. In terms of language and ethnic characteristics they are just as indistinguishable from Chinese as are Irish Catholics from Irish Protestants. This is certainly a sure sign of the strength of separatist tendencies in China.

Russian travelers who visited Manchuria at the turn of the century came back with the impression that the desire for autonomy was very much on the minds of the local Chinese population. The man who achieved that goal and indeed very nearly brought about Manchuria's complete secession from China was the ruler of Manchuria, Chang Tso-lin, himself a Han Chinese.

Eastern Turkestan is another area many of whose Chinese rulers made attempts to draw as far away as possible from the central government and even to break away from China. They include General Ma, Sheng Shih-tsai, and General Wang En-mao, who proved a very hard nut for Peking to crack.

A similar situation has been observed in Mongolia too. Chinese sources have noted that many Chinese settlers display solidarity with, and support for, the Mongols in their opposition to the central authority.

Some reports from Tibet have given grounds to believe that a tendency of the same kind is in evidence there too. Back in 1967 big-character posters in Peking had claimed an anti-Peking revolt led by General Chang Kuo-hua was underway in Tibet.

It would appear that two forces are at work in each of the national areas, both aimed at breaking away from China. They are, on the one hand, regional separatist tendencies represented by Han Chinese living in the territory concerned and, on the other, the aspirations of the local nationalities whose objective is independence. In many instances these two forces have come into contact although there have been no reported cases of fusion between them. For the central authorities, however, the combined results of their action undoubtedly add up to a serious problem.

"Once again," writes Klaus Menert in this connection, "the question is asked, as it was forty or fifty years ago, whether China is not on the point of decomposing into provinces under the control of individual generals who today rule large sections of the Empire as heads of the revolutionary committees."

The reference to linguistic diversity should be seen in the light of the fact that the process of absorption of local dialects by larger ones is still far from over in modern China. And, most important, out of the eight major dialects (Pekingese is but one of them), the principal ones are mutually unintelligible. There is thus no single nationwide language, which means, if we recall Stalin's famous definition of a nation, that one major characteristic of a single nation is missing.

There are several factors operating in favor of the centrifugal forces both in minority areas and in China proper. These are: (a) a certain economic self-containment of several provinces of China, (b) the historical traditions and the simultaneous existence of several Chinese states, [1] (c) the anti-Maoist ideological trends which Peking has so far been powerless to destroy, and (d) linguistic diversity.

---

[1] This is one of the psychological reasons why the Chinese find it so easy to accept the present-day reality of "two Chinas."

Similar doubts arise as to the existence in China of the other characteristics listed by Stalin, as together forming the concept of a nation. Notably, regional distinctions in the field of culture are so varied that unless the Pekingese court standards are accepted as a nationwide pattern, China can hardly be said to have any common cultural makeup—at any rate, no more than any of the no less fragmentarily made up African countries, or India, which likewise has no single nationwide language and which is only just moving toward the formation of a single nation. The administrative incorporation of various territories into one system may ultimately result in the fusion of different ethnic groups and the formation of a single nation. That process is at present underway in China. It is a slow process of the integration of different territorial communities, conventionally referred to as Han Chinese yet having no common language. As already mentioned above, Chinese living in different provinces cannot understand one another.

The separatist tendencies of individual Chinese military and political leaders reflect the trend of public opinion in those territories. Sometimes, these separatist tendencies take the form of enmity between the provinces. This traditional antagonism is in fact a historical echo of the forcible union of these adjacent territories around the Han people. Apart from this provincial antagonism the fact that the nation-building process has not yet been completed is also evidenced by the linguistic, ethnic, and anthropological patchwork structure of the various provinces.

Another characteristic point is the absence in China of the concept of patriotism in the sense of loyalty to, or preference for, one's own nation. Historically as well as now the Chinese concept of patriotism has never been anything more than loyalty to a ruler. In its time it was loyalty to the emperor, then loyalty to Mao, and today—loyalty to Hua Ko-feng. It is by the depth of personal loyalty and the ability to admire the leader that individual loyalty to the regime is measured. Thus the emotional connecting link between the Chinese is not their patriotism; instead it is their reaction to the personality of their ruler, a personified symbol of unity. This surely indicates that the very concept of nationhood has not yet been fully recognized within the framework of China's social consciousness. In its primitive stage, whatever awareness of nationhood there is will usually find expression not through positive but negative attitudes—for instance, through hostility to all that is alien and non-Chinese.

This typically Chinese attitude has been noted by many China-watchers, both past and present. Describing the Chinese treatment of foreigners, the Russian Archpriest Nikolai Dyakov wrote that the Chinese "gape at us and scorn us, while extolling all that is theirs." This deliberately negative attitude to all things not Chinese was also described with chagrined surprise by Grum-Grzhimailo: "Not a single kind look, not a single kind face will you see here. Expect no courtesies. Your question will go unanswered. But there will be boors who, while brazenly belching in your face, will begin investigating everything they see on you, and even your beard will not go untouched . . . and all this to the accompaniment of the choicest swear words and laughter, that wild and idiotic laughter."

This disdainful attitude to everything non-Chinese at the level of personal contacts spreads to the broader spheres of communication, such as international relations. Hence the emphatically scornful treatment not only of individual representatives of other nations but also of entire peoples and states. In their references to Russia, for instance, Chinese authors would always point out that this was "a barbarian state from Eastern Europe." In 1816 one Chinese commentator described Britain as "a single small barbarian state."

Numerous proofs of this disdainful attitude to other nations are provided by the diplomatic correspondence sent by Chinese rulers to foreign monarchs. This, for instance, is how Emperor Tsiang Lun replied to King George III of England. "We, by the grace of heaven, emperor, instruct the King of England to take note of our charge.

"Although your country, O King, lies in the far oceans, yet inclining your heart towards civilization you have specially sent an envoy respectfully to present a state message.

"Now you, O King, have presented various objects to the Throne and mindful of your loyalty we have specially ordered our ministry to receive them.

"Nevertheless we have never valued indigenous articles, nor do we have the slightest need of your country's manufacture. Therefore, O King, as regards your request to send someone to remain at the capital for trade, while it is not in harmony with the regulations of the Celestial Empire, we also feel very much that it is of no advantage to your country. Hence we have issued these detailed instructions and have commanded your tribute envoys to return safely home. You, O King, should simply act in conformity with our wishes by strengthening your loyalty and swearing perpetual obedience so as to ensure that your country may share the blessings of peace. . . ."

Such displays of the "arrogance and impudence of the Chinese Government" (the words belong to an early twentieth-century Russian author) are links in one and the same chain. They are more than a simple display of provincial delusion of grandeur. They are a product of the long and painful process of the development of national consciousness. And on the other hand, they are a proof of the absence of any national consciousness.

The absence of a united national (as distinct from state) consciousness undoubtedly facilitates the operation of centrifugal forces. In effect, the existence of such forces has already resulted in the appearance of the "other China" as an antipode to the Communist China. Certain facts and reports warrant the belief that ideological opposition to Peking exists in Mainland China too. Under favorable circumstances the opposition may one day take a concrete shape—politically, militarily, and perhaps even governmentally.

This is evidenced in particular by the broadcasts from Chinese territory of clandestine radio stations which pull no punches in their savage criticism of Maoist ideology. They include radio stations operating under titles like "Voice of the Liberation Army," "The Communist Party of China," "The Spark," "The Voice of Anti-Communism," and others. It is also evidenced by the appearance of underground handwritten and printed publications, notably the newspaper, *Polemic* in Shensi.

The list of factors strengthening the action of centrifugal forces in China proper does not end here. At different times, depending on the international situation and on the situation inside the country, some of those factors move up into the foreground while others recede into the sidelines. The important point is, however, that the very existence of forces threatening the country's unity was fully recognized by Chinese rulers long before Mao. The separatist tendencies of various Chinese provinces was a thorn in the side of both the Manchu emperors and the republican governments that succeeded them.

Unable to unite the entire Chinese territory under a single economic system, the rulers attempted to achieve that unity on the basis of common traditional forms of social consciousness—especially religion. This objective was also served by uniform standards of etiquette and standards governing the manner of dress and even the hairdos of the people. The slightest departure from this uniformity (such as a decision to part with the pigtail) was seen as a breach of loyalty to the imperial throne and was treated as a felony. The intensity of this never-ending campaign of regimentation is the measure of the strength of the regional centrifugal tendencies which it was designed to overcome.

The noted Russian explorer G.E. Grum-Grzhimailo recorded this curious observation about the significance of the regimented mentality in China: "Are they not bound to dress, live, even bow, eat, drink, sleep and think in a manner that has been laid down for them once and for all? Where, in what other country or state could the depersonalization of people have gone so far? China!? . . . This is what it really is: it is a vast land of mannequins, where people will fall flat on their faces before you when ordered to do so for some reason by the authorities or else revile you if another string is pulled."

Though written a good eighty years ago, these remarks read like an eyewitness account of the state of affairs in China today. The rigorously imposed regimentation of the public mind is indeed a Chinese tradition of long-standing—and one which may well provide the key to the depressingly uniform behavior of modern Chinese which never stops baffling the European observer. Commenting on the stereotyped conformity of Chinese mass psychology, the Buryat scholar P.A. Badmayev had this to say: "Such an inert mass can always be aroused and guided in any direction. . . . They will always be a plaything in the hands of the clever predators." This is, surely, a most up-to-date observation, though actually written in the last century.

The cult of Mao may also be seen as a measure aimed at regimenting the mentality of the people. The very need for such regimentation may in turn be regarded as an indirect indication of the existence of sufficiently strong countercurrents, both regional and separatist.

The eulogizing and deification of Mao in his time have long since overstepped the limits of anything that might have been dictated by the need to assert his authority and personal power. The striking part is the purely ritualistic aspect of the act of worship which is steadily upstaging every other conceivable aspect. A clearly defined pattern of Mao worship was molded during the Cultural Revolution. Its principal element was the observance of an established ritual which includes such forms of illusory activity as the writing of big-character posters, the copying out of quotations and sayings, and the recitation of quotations. The Soviet researcher A.N. Zhelokhovtsev has mentioned such characteristically religious features of the Mao cult as the cult of miracles (reports of miraculous cures and alleged facts of mass reeducation—the deaf and dumb begin to sing in chorus, a thieving shop girl returns her loot after reading some selected quotations). Also in this category is the system of collective confessions which is almost identical to the Christian institution of church confession. In the course of this ritual of worship the individual dissolves, as it were, in the common spiritual medium designed to unite all and sundry into one uniform mass. "When all Chinese," writes Klaus Menert, "spend 30 minutes or an hour (if not more) a day in communal recitation from the Mao bible, this is also a uniting link, quite independent of whether individuals agree with the sayings or inwardly reject them."

Mao's death has brought no changes to this mechanism. The cult of the living Mao was replaced by the cult of the dead Mao, completely infallible in death. Meanwhile Mao's successor, Hua Ko-feng has a cult of his own growing like a sapling in the shadow of the cult of Mao. In present-day China Hua's name is invariably linked with the epithet "wise" but this positive psychological reality is bound to have a negative pole, a pole of alienation. So at the other end of the scale we have Liu Shao-chi, then Lin Piao, and later the "gang of four," the symbols of all that is "bad," "reactionary," and "revisionist." This symbol is also based on the principle of maximum simplifications and, therefore, it too is easily identified by even the most primitive intellect.

The two polarities—Mao, the force of light, and the forces of darkness notwithstanding the personification—serve in equal measure the single purpose of achieving the emotional consolidation of the countless Chinese millions.

It is reasonable to assume that the individual qualities of the living prototypes of these two symbols are not of the slightest consequence. It would have taken no more than a different alignment of political forces at some point in the past for each of them to go down in history in the other's place.

It is hard to tell whether the development of this unifying dualistic alignment of good and evil in the social consciousness was a result of deliberate action or of the spontaneous reaction of social forces. Whatever the answer may be, the unifying aim of the China's leader cult is as plain as can be. But it can also be regarded as an indirect sign of the existence of an opposing force, to defeat which the whole idea was conceived.

## The Uncertain Future

In the future I see two things that will strengthen the forces straining to break up China: the population explosion and the explosive military and political situation.

Living in the world of today, we often find it hard even to imagine that fairly recently, in 1886, China's population was a mere 123 million. In 1964, in a conversation with the American author, the late Edgar Snow, Mao Tse-tung replied to his question about China's population by saying that some people think it is between 680 and 690 million; however, several years later it was estimated at 700 million. In 1976 the Japanese news agency Kyodo analyzed the cables which came from various provinces and towns of China on the occasion of Mao's death. These contained data on the numerical strength of China's population and, according to Kyodo, the total population had reached 891 million. However, at the end of 1977 the *Far Eastern Review,* the Hong Kong weekly, already quoted a figure of one thousand million people. The same estimate is made by Harrison Salisbury in his book *War Between Russia and China.* It is indeed generally predicted that by the year 2000 China's total population will rise to somewhere between 1.5 and 2 billion.

The prospect of a swiftly rising population in the limited land space of China is reminiscent of what happens with a steam boiler: An unchecked increase in pressure is bound to result in an explosion. So far the role of safety valves helping to keep the population pressure under some measure of control has been played by the outlying minority areas into which settlers from the central areas of the country have been continuously streaming in their millions. But for one thing, the outlying areas themselves also have a certain critical limit to their intake capacity. For another, those Chinese who settle in these remote lands with their historically loose bonds with China proper, themselves become exponents not only of regional but also of clearly defined separatist tendencies.

Until lately Peking itself did not seem to be very worried about the population increase becoming a factor which might add strength to the forces working toward the breakup of China. The population growth was therefore treated from the traditional standpoint as a factor promoting stronger central authority and as a potential reserve for future territorial expansion. This way of looking at it may, however, be a result of the failure of population-control projects. It is indeed very much like the Chinese Communists to declare a negative and uncontrollable situation to be a favorable and radiant one. Peking's recent position has been rather aptly described by a Chinese author as follows: "A large population becomes a very important factor in promoting the rapid development of the national economy and culture. Under such circumstances, the larger the population is, the greater, faster, better and more economic will be socialist construction. . . ."

Lately, however, there have been signs that Peking is beginning to review her position. In the summer of 1977 *Jenmin Jihpao* (the *People's Daily*) carried a statement by Chou En-lai to the effect that a one-percent reduction in the rate of growth of the population would be most desirable. The paper cited the positive experience of some provinces where this has been achieved. In the same year an all-China conference on the reduction of the birthrate was held in Peking. Young people were asked to postpone marriage until they were twenty-five and those already married were advised to limit their families to one or two children. It is difficult to say whether these measures will prove effective but China-watchers report that already in 1977 China had the world's lowest birthrate—six births per thousand.

Whatever the considerations behind this turn in demographic policy, they most certainly included apprehension of the danger which uncontrolled population growth might spell for the unity of China.

The other factor also menacing the integrity of China is the likelihood of crisis-fraught situations. Historical parallels both with czarist Russia and with imperial China indicate that sufficiently powerful onslaughts on the foundations of central authority inevitably lead to separatist explosions. In Russia the downfall of imperial authority was immediately followed by the secession of Poland, Finland, Latvia, Estonia, and Lithuania. The Ukraine declared its independence. Georgia made an attempt to break away. Even the Russian-inhabited Far East severed its ties with central Russia and formed the Far Eastern Republic. The same thing happened in China. Hardly had the Ching dynasty fallen when Mongolia and Tibet declared their independence and Eastern Turkestan and Manchuria stepped up their own struggle to break away from China.

To the extent that Byron's words that the past is prologue to the future are applicable to history, there are good reasons to expect that the rigid connection between sociopolitical upheavals and a strengthening of separatist tendencies will be just as strong in the future as it has been in the past. As the Soviet political periodical *Novoye Vremya (New Times)* pointed out, "The considerable collapse of central authority and the increase of separatist tendencies could become particularly dangerous if the tradition of Chinese history is taken into consideration: In critical moments, the unified state has split into separate parts."

The likelihood of entire provinces seceding from China has not been ruled out by Klaus Menert who also bases supposition on the development of crisis-fraught situations.

Not only crisis-fraught, however. In *Issues and Studies* published in Taipei, R. Starr, citing the analysis of China's economic and political situation made by the Joint Economics Committee of the U.S. Congress and a group of experts of the Hoover Institute, offers this projection of China's development: China will most likely be still further decentralized, with several almost independent and autonomous regions being set up on the basis of some of the bigger military districts. The historical separatist trends which have rent China asunder from time immemorial may well turn out to be realized by the military command of those districts which have concentrated enormous authority in their hands after the Cultural Revolution.

In China itself this foreign-born prognosis can hardly be anything like a revelation. Mao Tse-tung and his entourage were doubtless aware of that danger. Hence the measures they took to prevent the concentration of too much power in the hands of the military. Especially in the outlying and national regions. To that end they did their best to vest that power in the hands of the party functionaries—ranging them against the military men in the process. This policy of prudence is continued by Mao's successors as well. The struggle which ensued after Mao's death—and which is still going on—proceeds by the removal of the military from all key positions of political power. And, first and foremost, in the border and minorities' districts.

Characteristically, Russian sinologists of the last century have also noted that simultaneous attacks against central authority inside the country and in its outlying national areas could result in the disintegration of China as a state. Referring to the events of the 1860s in China, A. Geins wrote at the time: "It is highly probable that we are at present attending the break-up into two parts of that vast political body which but recently occupied the entire central and eastern parts of Asia."

Obviously, the survival of China's unity is a life or death problem for the Chinese state—at least in its present form. This is what explains the amazing unanimity in this issue of the Chinese Communists and the Nationalists. This, too, explains the evolution in the views of both groups, ranging from recognition of the rights of the nationalities incorporated in China to secession all the way to a complete denial of that right.

In 1924 Sun Yat-sen wrote in the manifesto of the 1st Chinese Nationalist Congress: "The Kuomintang solemnly declares that the right of self-determination is recognized for all the nationalities inhabiting China; following the victory of the revolution over the imperialists and militarists there will be established a free and united (formed on the basis of a voluntary union of all nationalities) Chinese republic." Later this policy was completely abandoned by the Kuomintang—both in theory and in practice.

We can observe the same evolution in the Chinese Communist views on this matter. The Constitution of the Chinese Soviet Republic adopted in November 1931 declared: "Soviet government in China recognizes the right of self-determination of the national minorities in China, their right to complete separation from China, and to the formation of an independent state for each national minority. Thus, the Mongols, Moslems, Tibetans, Koreans and others inhabiting the territory of China enjoy the complete right to self-determination, that is, they may either join the Union of Chinese Soviets or secede from it and form their own state as they may prefer."

Early manifestoes of the Chinese Communist party also stick to this position. Paragraph 3 of the Action Program adopted by the 6th Congress of the Chinese Communist party was in fact titled "The Unification of China and Recognition of the Right to National Self-Determination." The preamble to the Communist party statute adopted by the 7th Congress also declared that the Communist party of China was struggling for the creation of a Chinese People's Federative Republic. In 1945 Mao Tse-tung wrote in his work, "On a Coalition Government," that the future People's China would "grant nations the right to be their own master and to voluntarily enter into an alliance with the Han people."

That was the last time the right to self-determination was mentioned. What is more, with Mao's elevation to the rank of undisputed ruler, all that had previously been said on behalf of the Chinese Communist party about self-determination was most rigorously censored and "corrected." In the political report to the 7th Congress Mao had stated: "All national minorities in China must create, along voluntary and democratic lines, a federation of democratic republics of China." In the later edition of Mao's *Selected Works* that passage has vanished without trace. The same report had originally listed a demand for the "granting of the right to national self-determination to all national minorities." In later editions these words were replaced with the phrase "the granting of the right to national autonomy to all national minorities."

The federation and self-determination slogans certainly appealed to the national minorities and, therefore, they were pragmatically advanced in the initial phase, in the interests of the anti-Kuomintang struggle. But as soon as victory was theirs Mao and his associates immediately jettisoned them and proceeded to turn China into a unitary state.

There are indications, however, that some of the smaller minorities came up against serious difficulties in attempts to achieve even a measure of autonomy. At any rate, the Chinese authorities certainly lost no opportunity to block any such move. Some provincial party leaders qualified the desire of the minorities for autonomy as "nationalism" and asserted that autonomy could be granted only when the local economy, finances, culture, and national personnel had attained an adequate level of development.

Almost immediately after Mao came to power some of his associates began cultivating the idea that the federal or Soviet method of resolving the national problem was unacceptable for China. This attitude was expressed in an article by Sha-Toh, "On the Forms and Extent of Regional National Autonomy in the People's Republic of China," which was published in the Chinese press. "If we say," the article points out, "that the forms and extent of the development of our regional autonomy may be similar to the Soviet pattern, this means recognising the eventuality of their becoming autonomous republics, or by logically extending that concept, the various nationalities of our country may obtain the right to form separate states, and the national autonomous regions may secede. Thus, as regards the forms and extent of regional autonomy in our country such a concept would run counter to the spirit of the Constitution and is, of course, erroneous."

It is this fear that the minority-populated areas might one day drop out that compels the Chinese leaders to rob them—and quite openly—of the last vestiges of autonomy. "The national autonomy existing in China is temporary and eventually it will be liquidated," Chou En-lai declared publicly in 1968.

These were not mere words. They were followed by deeds. Soon afterwards Kang Ming, a leading official of the Nationalities' Affairs Committee, declared that national autonomy was altogether inapplicable under Chinese conditions. According to his concept, the national minorities do not dwell on their own territory anyway but on alien, that is, Chinese territory. And since they certainly have no right to dispose of someone else's property as they see fit, they consequently cannot have any autonomy. Therefore the principle of national autonomy and self-determination has no future in China.

The last remaining step to be taken was the formalization de jure of the lawlessness that had been observed de facto and no time was lost. In the autumn of 1975 China adopted a new constitution which in effect reduced the autonomous regions to ordinary rank and file administrative entities. Its 1978 constitution brought no improvement.

The only thing now left of what used to be a program of minority development is the word "autonomous." Robbed of all meaning, it has lost its raison d'être—and it is perhaps this that gives the Chinese leaders no cause to hurriedly drop it altogether.

It is certainly Mao and his followers, more than any of the political groups that preceded them, who have had to cope with breakaway and secessionist tendencies in China. Small wonder that it is they who have been making the greatest effort to obliterate them.

According to signs coming from China recently, Hua Ko-feng and his supporters are concerned about this problem to no less a degree. There are reasons to suppose that Mao's successors will go further in this direction than the Chairman himself. The growing tendencies to separation inevitably incur stronger measures on the part of the central government to control them.

# 6

# CHAINED

In the last century the French prognosticator Charles Richet wrote a book prophetically entitled *Dans Cent Ans (A Hundred Years Hereafter)*. He predicted that one century after his time China would not only push the Europeans out of Asia but would also become the dominant colonial power. But the new colonialists would be not just "temporary victors," but assimilators who "would universally inject into the vanquished people their mores, their industry, and their language." Today, in the example of China's national borderlands, we can see that prediction gradually coming true.

The theoretical attitude of the Chinese Communists to the self-determination of nations had gone all the way from one extreme, recognition of the right of nations to self-determination, to the other, complete denial of that right. A matching road of evolution, where the end position is the very opposite of the starting position, has been traveled by the practices of the Chinese Communists in the national question as well.

The initial phase was keynoted by the proclamation of a principle completely favoring the non-Han nationalities in China.

In the process of implementing the initial position, the First All-China Congress of Soviets announced the goal of putting an end forever to national oppression by granting all national minorities full equality with the Han Chinese in all fields of public life.

Addressing the 6th Expanded Plenary Meeting of the Central Committee of the Chinese Communist party in 1938, Mao Tse-tung emphasized the need to grant national minorities equal rights with the Han and declared that they should have their own administration, while the Han Chinese should respect the culture, religion, and traditions of the national minorities and promote their cultural growth and development of their native languages.

This line was repeated by Mao at the 7th Congress of the Chinese Communist party in April 1945, where he said: "The spoken and written language, the rights, customs, and religious beliefs of the national minorities must be respected."

But at the time Mao was uttering those words it was quite impossible to imagine that several years later the Chinese press would have banner headlines with directly opposite appeals. But that is exactly what happened—and without much delay. It was proclaimed from the rostrum of the very first session of the Assembly of People's Representatives that "politically, economically, and culturally the Chinese stand considerably higher than the other nationalities of our country."

This statement was surely tantamount to saying that one nationality was by no means equal but far superior to all the others. But it was still only a forerunner of what was to come. And that was the thesis of the necessity and the desirability of the elimination of all other nationalities except for the Chinese. "The Chinese constitute 94 percent of the entire population of China," reported the magazine *Sinkiang Hung Chi* in 1960, "and from the viewpoint of political, economic, and cultural development they are the more advanced. Therefore the fusion of nationalities must come about on the basis of one nationality. In the context of China it is the Chinese who must form that backbone."

"This fusion," stated the newspaper *Sinkiang Jih Pao (Sinkiang Red Flag),* "is a Marxist and Communist assimilation and an inevitable tendency of the development of society. Those who are opposed to such assimilation oppose Socialism and Communism; they oppose historical materialism."

By way of carrying out in practice the principle set forth above, ever since 1958 representatives of all the national minorities were instructed to address all conferences, congresses, and other gatherings only in Chinese.

This was certainly in marked contrast to the appeal for the equality of other nationalities and for the development of their language, culture, and self-government. It was a line aimed at the assimilation, disappearance, and virtual extinction of the non-Han minorities in China. "The distinctions of the Chinese nation," *Sinkiang Hung Chi* summarized, "will turn into the common national distinctions of the national minorities."

This was the signal for a transition to a nationalities policy that was the very opposite of all that had previously been declared. Having caught the chicken, the farmer's wife made no more clucking noises. She reached for her knife.

According to the account of one former Chinese ideological functionary who fled to the USSR some time ago, the official interpretation put on these developments by party officials who deal with national issues is this: It is asserted that the other nationalities making up China are nothing but branches of the Han nation and that the basic task is to bring them all back into the family fold. From this standpoint, not only the present-day assimilation policy but also the preceding phase (that is, the annexations and conquests practiced by the Chinese emperors), appear altogether justified and fair. Indeed, one has only to look into *Chung Kuo Duan Shi (The Short History of China)*, published in Peking, to find a great many arguments emphasizing the justice of incorporating into China Eastern Turkestan, Tibet, Burma, Vietnam, Nepal, and all other neighboring countries and peoples. "The unification policy of the Ching State," says one publication, "has created favorable opportunities for the economic and cultural drawing together of many nationalities."

Having gone back on their former promises and policies, the Peking leaders did their best to make a clean break with those whose names had been associated with that policy. Thus, the initial soft line toward the non-Han nationalities was directly associated in the official Chinese press with the detrimental line of the "revisionist" Liu Shao-chi, "who had granted the nationalities too much freedom."

The Peking press branded the advocates of the "soft line" as "men of the Chinese Khrushchev," charging them in particular with "believing that it was possible to take into account the specific features of the regions and that the policy pursued inside the country should not be applied in those regions."

According to Western press reports, Liu Chun, Vice-Chairman of the National Minorities Committee of the Council of State, had mapped out the political line of the future in 1964. Under this new policy, all public and religious leaders were slated to be gradually eased out of the picture. The basic task was economic and cultural uniformity in order to attain a fusion of nationalities and the gradual obliteration of national distinctions.

Though Liu Chun and his associates were themselves eased out of the picture in 1966, the seeds they had sown fell on fertile soil and yielded a rich harvest.

Peking's offensive against the national areas was based on the five-column principle—almost like Franco's army in its advance on Madrid. Four of these acted in the open. They were (1) the dismemberment of the nationalities, (2) the liquidation of national cadres and the intelligentsia, (3) reprisals, and (4) the mass-scale Chinese resettlement of the national areas.

As in Franco's case, the fifth column penetrated and operated inside the enemy camp. It was made up of representatives of the local people who had adopted, or were willing to adopt, the way of life, the thoughts, and the language that were being imposed upon them by the Han colonizers. Esau, who sold his birthright for a mess of pottage, had his followers. There were not many, it is true, and it was Peking's aim to increase their number many times over.

Some researchers and travelers who visited China in the past noted several instances of such voluntary assimilation. For instance, A. Screen, a British Consul in Eastern Turkestan, wrote that during his sojourn in that country he had several times heard of Turki people who had "embraced the Chinese culture, at least in its external aspect, and who held various administrative offices." "On our way," he wrote, "we met two so to say 'sinified' natives. They were Moslems from Hotang, but for the sake of a career and to gain more profitable administrative positions they had adopted the Chinese manners, speech and attire."

In referring to the four columns, I singled out four elements in Peking's assimilation drive.

1. *The dismemberment of nationalities.* The dismemberment of na-

tionalities and their consignment to various administrative entities is well illustrated by the examples of Mongolia, Eastern Turkestan, and Tibet. Apart from Inner Mongolia proper, the Mongols have been dispersed throughout another eight autonomous *chous* and districts incorporated in other provinces. Apart from Tibet, Tibetans are to be found in nine autonomous *chous* and two autonomous districts which, though directly bordering on Tibet, do not form part of it but are divided between other provinces. "The Mao Tse-tung group," writes a Soviet orientologist in this connection, "has in fact dismembered the Tibetan people."

The Kazakhs have been split up among three autonomous districts and one *chou*. The Miaos live in four different autonomous districts incorporated in various provinces. Three and one-half million Huis make up eight different autonomous districts incorporated in the provinces of Kansu, Tsinghai, Yunnan, Inner Mongolia, and Sinkiang.

The Chuangs, like many other lesser minorities, live in a compact mass on a common territory. This naturally creates a possibility for their consolidation as a nation. This is why Peking has done its best to divide the Chuangs among the provinces of Kwangsi, Kweichow, and Kwangtung. What is more, in Kweichow one group of Chuangs has artificially been isolated into a separate nationality called Bui. If all the Chuangs were united within a single adminstrative unit its total population would be over 10 million. The important thing is that this people has a strong tradition of statehood going all the way back to the third century A.D. and that among the Chuangs themselves there is a strong urge to unite. In 1957 Professor Huan Hsiang-fang, himself a Chuang, reflected their mood in this fairly cautious and streamlined way: "We believe that the peoples making up the Chuang group, who have a single language and identical customs, will gradually come to an awareness that they belong to the Chuang nation, with the result that the population of the autonomous *chou* will continuously grow and its territory increase."

This one sentence from the professor's *Short History of the Kuangsi Chuangs* proved more than enough for his book to be banned and for the learned scholar himself to be fired from the university with the stamp of "nationalist" all over him. Recalling all the headaches which the other secession-minded minorities have caused them, the Peking authorities are least of all interested in anything of the kind ever happening, for the Chuangs would then become the biggest of the country's non-Han minorities. Yes, this is exactly what did happen—and very soon too. It was loudly declared from the rostrum of the first session of the People's Congress that "politically, economically, and culturally, the Chinese stand considerably higher than the other nationalities of our country."

This was no longer a declaration of equality, it was a declaration of the superiority of one nation over all the others. But this was merely the premise for the fundamental conclusion which was to come.

The policy of cutting up nations into pieces—which has been pursued for quite a long time—is bearing fruit. The Soviet scholar R.F. Its has noted that the Yis, who used to be a closely-knit people, were in the middle of the twentieth century split into two completely isolated groupings of highlanders (in Liangshan) and plainsmen (in Yunnan). Similarly, the Miaos have lost their former unity and broken up into several geographical and ethnical groups.

The American researcher Douglas Jackson has justly pointed out that the Chinese are deliberately splitting up various national groups to block their consolidation. "The 'autonomy' practiced in China," a Soviet author has recently emphasized, "is nothing but a fragmentation of nationalities, a forcible and artificial break-up of their historically formed ethnical boundaries."

It is hardly necessary to explain that such action, which slows down the development of the national consciousness of ethnical groups and nations, makes it much easier to assimilate them.

2. *Liquidation of national leaders and intellectuals.* Liu Chun's program which called for the removal of local leaders gained particular momentum during the Cultural Revolution. It was preceded by a fairly protracted period in which potential national leaders were singled out and slated for promotion. Under Article 12 of the Basic Principles and Article 68 of the Constitution of the Chinese People's Republic, organs of self-government in all national autonomous regions were supposed to be made up of persons belonging to the local nationality. Chinese authors writing about the nationalities question at the time were unanimous in emphasizing how essential it was to carry this policy through. "The training of national cadres," one of them wrote, "and their gradual inclusion into the organs of self-government and leading party organs constitutes the main link determining the entire

work of the Party in the national regions." "It is necessary," another author stressed, "to strive to gradually impart a national character to the autonomous organs of government, which constitutes the very essence of the policy of local national autonomy."

The Chinese paper, *Chen Fang Tsun Pao (Liberation Army Daily)*, reported at the time that "the imparting of a national character to the organs of self-government is the central question of the policy of implementing local national autonomy."

Judging by some Chinese press reports, however, even in that period everything was not as smooth as it seemed. Some party functionaries and administrative officers tried to block the recruitment of national personnel into the machinery of self-government. Another flaw was the fact that the Han-populated territories enjoyed a higher level of popular representation than the norm established in minority regions.

Nonetheless, on the whole, the initial period of the existence of People's China was characterized by the elevation of national personnel to leading positions in the autonomous territories.

Looking back, this elevation of national officials may be regarded as a deliberate—and highly successful—effort to earmark the exponents of nationalist tendencies who were then slated for swift elimination. The actual process of elimination—also thanks to measures taken well in advance—passed far less painfully for the national communities than it would had none of those measures been taken. Throughout the country, but especially in the minority areas, party organs had been set up as a parallel system of power. In contrast to the bodies of local self-government, the party committees were made up mostly of Han Chinese, usually party functionaries appointed by Peking. In accordance with the standard Marxist concept of the leading and guiding role of the party, the party committees began increasingly to take over the leading policymaking functions, while the local organs of government were left with little more than executive duties.

So when the national leaders began losing their jobs—and often their heads too—their administrative functions were promptly taken over by the predominantly Han-staffed party committees. In this process cultural and art workers are being persecuted and national autonomy rights infringed. Many leaders of autonomous regions with local nationalities have been removed from their posts and declared enemies. Persons of Chinese nationality have been placed at the head of the revolutionary committees in all five autonomous regions.

The elimination of national minority leaders from public life has now gone so far that at the opening of the 9th Congress of the Chinese Communist party not one of the delegates of Tibet, Inner Mongolia, and Eastern Turkestan was elected to the Congress presidium. This was noted and widely commented on by Western observers.

3. *Outright reprisals against the national minorities.* This theme has been discussed in some detail in the preceding chapters which dealt with the problems of the main minority groups separately. Here I merely want to emphasize the tradition of the physical elimination of other ethnic groups as a method of solving the nationalities problem in China and to provide some of the facts relating to the number of victims among the people of the minority areas in recent years.

In the eighteenth century the Chinese carried out what amounted to the wholesale massacre of the Huis. Grum-Grzhimailo describes that event as something "unprecedented in the history of the East." Only a few thousand Huis survived by crossing the Sino-Russian frontier and seeking refuge in Russia. The rest of the population, inhabiting a territory bigger than France in size, was completely destroyed. This method of physically eliminating, or else artificially creating conditions for the extinction of, lesser minority groups in present-day China should on no account be underestimated. This is particularly true if you take into account the total absence of publicity and the consequent possibility of throwing a cloak of secrecy over events taking place in remote areas of the country. Not for nothing does the Chinese language have a set phrase, "to drive into the mountains," which is usually applied to national minorities.

The idea of achieving the ultimate unity of China through the wiping out or extinction of "alien" national groups rests on a solid foundation. According to the Indian demographer, Amrit Lal, the result of this policy has been that the proportion of national minorities decreased from 6.6 percent to 5 percent between 1953 and 1962. And since 1949 the proportion of the national minorities in China has dropped by half, plummeting from 10 to 5 percent. Considering the millions of human lives crammed into these percentages the decline is a staggering one.

This process of gradual extinction is also reflected in the falling birthrate in the minority areas. The average annual population increase for Han Chinese is 2.4 percent; for the four main non-Han minorities it is only 0.9 percent.

A simple exercise in arithmetic will show that if this rate of decline in the proportion of the national minorities persists, it will take just three decades for their share in China's population to drop below the one-percent mark, that is, to become virtually nonexistent.

If there is anything at all that Peking does not like about this method of finally bringing about China's national unity, it is the time involved. Mao and his entourage evidently feel they do not have that much time at their disposal. The gradual method would put off for too long the achievement of Peking's other objectives—and this it can never accept. This is why the idea of a steady physical extermination is coming to the fore, although it is, of course, combined with the other measures we have been discussing.

The output of steel and the yields of rice constitute a state secret in China but an even more closely guarded secret is information about the number of people put to death in the minority areas during the reign of the Maoists. Some figures have nonetheless found their way into the press. Chou En-lai has stated that since the victory of the Chinese Communist regime "about 2 million bandits were executed in China" by early 1953. This gives an average of between 600,000 and 700,000 a year. Even in conditions of political stability, the same steady rate of extermination would by now have yielded a bloody harvest of between 12 and 14 million.

But the period that followed the date named by Chou En-lai was by no means a period of stability. It was a time of colonizing wars in Mongolia, Tibet, and Eastern Turkestan. So the number of victims could not have remained at the former level. The press has given the following figures: 13 million killed in 1961–1965 and 5 million in 1966–1967.

The Soviet professor F. Zaporozhsky has given a figure of 25 million as the total number of purge victims from 1955 to 1965.

These figures seem to be sufficiently close to the truth. It is, however, most unlikely that Peking will release any more accurate information—not only because of the secrecy surrounding such figures, which we have already mentioned, but also because the Chinese themselves probably have no such figures at hand. Indeed, if Mao himself admitted that he was not in possession of any reliable figures on the number of his living subjects, why should Peking bother to count the dead ones?

What then is the proportion of minorities among the victims of the campaign of terror in China? I have no ready answer. But logic prompts the assumption that the distribution of those victims between the Han and the non-Han Chinese should be in direct ratio to the resistance they each put up. Since the brunt of the struggle in this period has centered on the outlying national territories, it would be correct to assume that over half the victims belonged to the non-Han minorities.

The loss of between 10 and 12 million people out of 42 million means in fact the loss of a quarter of the total minority population of China. In purely demographical terms alone such losses must have been a truly crippling blow for the national minorities.

4. *Peking's resettlement policy.* The main targets of Peking's population expansion are the outlying minority-populated areas. Prior to 1949 these areas—Inner Mongolia, Tibet, and Eastern Turkestan—were mainly populated by non-Han peoples. Today, however, the Chinese are in the majority even there.

Objects of Peking's special concern are the southern provinces which today hold the bulk of the country's non-Han population—altogether 26 million people. Because of their traditional introverted way of life these peoples were until now almost immune to assimilation by Chinese culture. Today the barriers are beginning to fall.

The fate of the almost totally nonexistent Manchu is now in store for the southern minorities of China, as well as for Mongolia, Tibet, and Turkestan, all of which, like Manchuria, have been subjected to a many-million-strong influx of Chinese resettlers. They are destined to follow in the footsteps of the already extinct non-Han peoples of southern China. The non-Han kingdoms of Yueh and Wu, the Dunyueh and Minyueh of Chekiang and Fukien, the "southern and southwestern barbarians" of the ancient Chinese chronicles all vanished centuries ago, engulfed by the tidal wave of Chinese immigrants.

Commenting on the results of China's resettlement policy, the Russian scholar A. Ya. Maximov wrote, "the Chinese government is displaying remarkable energy, a wonderful talent for colonisation and great aptitude for swiftly attaining its objectives."

These words, written at the turn of the century, are more than to the point today, when the migration policy aimed at assimilating the non-Chinese nationalities has been elevated to the status of a national objective.

Though written at the start of this century these words can be echoed with even greater justification today when the resettlement policy designed to assimilate the non-Han peoples has virtually been proclaimed a national task.

Obviously anticipating this finale, the new Chinese Communist Party Rules, unlike previously, has not a single word to say either about the existence of the nationalities question or about the presence in China of any nationalities other than Han.

Peking's migration policies are coming up against natural resistance. As the noted Indian demographer Subhash Chandra Sarker has pointed out: "The government has sought to encourage large-scale resettlement in minority areas, but it is opposed not only by the patent unwillingness of the Chinese to move out of a familiar environment to face an uncertain future, but also by the unconcealed distrust of Chinese intentions, sometimes amounting to active hostility of the minorities, who cherish bitter memories of past Chinese oppression."

This hostility is reinforced by the fact that Communist Chinese are pursuing the same policy of extermination and assimilation in the minority areas as the Kuomintang Chinese. By this token, in the minds of the national minorities, the very word "Chinese" becomes a symbol of evil: There simply cannot be a bad or a good Chinese—the Chinese is always an enemy.

But this understandable and natural opposition is powerless to alter the course of, or slow down, what is already happening. The influx of Chinese resettlers into the minority areas will doubtless continue, unless, of course, it is interrupted by events of greater significance and strength than the impotent opposition of local nationalities or the inertia of those Chinese who are unwilling to move out of a familiar environment.

———

China is locked in battle with a dragon that wants to tear it asunder. The outcome is still unpredictable. Peking is making a superhuman effort to kill the dragon and subdue the centrifugal forces threatening the unity of China. But the dragon is still dangerous. Even if perhaps it cannot tear out a hunk of China's territory, for the moment, it can still prevent Peking from moving ahead with its expansionist plans. But the very nature of the present regime in China is such that it can exist only if it is not static, only if it is in motion, and only in an atmosphere of "world historic" victories and triumphs.

This is because, having declared itself to be the antithesis of "static" Soviet Communism, Chinese Communism has thereby doomed itself to the inexorable need constantly to assert its right to exist by continuously demonstrating its political dynamism and its drive toward world revolution. This has become the ideological condition for its very right to exist. In this respect it is like a bicycle which stays upright only in motion: As soon as it stops, it falls over—together with the cyclist.

# 7

# AGGRESSION TO
# THE NORTH

## Out for Soviet Territory

The territory that Peking is claiming with no holds barred is the Maritime Region—the area furthest away from Russia's European portion. Far back in the late fifties the Wuhan newspaper *Chantsin jih pao* pointed out that the Maritime Province butted against China, was a part of Chinese territory, and should, therefore, be returned to China.

The more far-extending Chinese claims are not limited to the Far East. Way back in the last century, during negotiations with the Russian government the Chinese representative insisted that Lake Baikal should be the border. "All that lies to the west of the lake is part of Russia, and all that lies to the east is part of China." At that time the lack of any arguments in favor of so unexpected a demand did, it is true, compel the Chinese side to give it up. But in 1925–1926 the militarist clique that was in power in China at the time again demanded that the Soviet–Chinese border be pushed back to the Baikal.

Only too logically, China, which continued the Ching policies in domestic affairs, pursued them in foreign affairs as well. So on July 10,

1964, Mao told a group of Japanese Socialist party parliamentarians: "There are too many places occupied by the Soviet Union. . . . Something like a hundred years ago the area east of the Baikal became the territory of Russia and since then Vladivostok, Khabarovsk, Kamchatka, and other localities have been the territory of the Soviet Union. We have not yet presented our check against that list."

For that matter several Chinese authors lay claim to areas that go much further than the Baikal. Some of them, such as Liu Shi, mention a boundary between China and Russia somewhere "to the west of the Ural Mountains." In his words, the lands east of the Urals should belong to China because they used to be part of the possessions of the ancient Chinese tribes of Hsianby and Huns.

Mention of the Huns gives the Chinese side a brilliant excuse to expand the limits of their territorial claims still further—all the way up to Western Europe and Italy.

The demand for a revision of the northern boundaries is fully backed by the Chinese press. For instance, in March 1963, *Jenmin Jihpao* (the *People's Daily*) had thrown doubts on the treaties under which almost all the present boundary between Russia and China was originally established. In 1964 the Chinese magazine of the theory of history, *Li-Shih Yen-chiu (Historical Research)*, printed an article by Liu Ta-nien which made an attempt to justify China's "historical rights" to vast territories of the Soviet Union. In the "Short Essay on Chinese Geography" by Jen Yu-ti, published in Peking in late 1964, a map was featured which marked off as "undefined state boundaries" sizable sections of the Sino-Soviet frontier in the Pamirs and along the Argun and Amur rivers. This is not the only map of its kind. Some maps issued in China have shown the boundary with the Soviet Union to be several hundred kilometers inside Russian territory.

The events on Damansky Island showed very clearly precisely how Mao intends to present those accounts. But the idea of a war with Russia to gain the Siberian territories was frequently advanced by Chinese nationalist and imperial circles long ago. Characteristic in this regard is a publication that appeared in Shanghai at the beginning of the century. The author tried to predict the most likely outcome of such a war. In his view, the Russian forces would sustain an ignominious defeat and fall back behind Irkutsk. The Chinese armies would then triumphantly occupy Vladivostok and the Maritime

Provinces would thereby become a Chinese possession. Thereafter all traces of a Russian presence on the shores of the Pacific were to be erased.

In the past such printed and public statements constituted a source of the subsequent military conflict and today such statements are preparing the ground for new armed clashes in the future. Even when on May 24, 1969, the Chinese government agreed to recognize the present boundary on a "basis" for the settlement of its claims, this was not in fact a recognition of the boundary, but another form of its denial. For the statement especially points out that the Chinese government is guided not by legal or historical circumstances but only by the fact that "broad masses of working people of the Soviet Union have for a long time been living in those places." Similar in content was the Chinese government statement on October 7, 1969. It again referred to territories belonging to China and "detached by czarist Russia with the help of unequal treaties." In other words, it was emphasized that though legally untenable, the situation continued only with the condescension and consent of the Chinese.

Soviet Central Asia, no less than Siberia and the Maritime Province, is an object of China's territorial claims. And they are claims with a long history behind them. Way back, after the conquest of Eastern Turkestan, China promptly began preparing to gobble up its other half. But rumors of the impending conquest, as one historian put it, "alarmed the entire Moslem world." The local Central Asian rulers decided to unite their efforts, while the powerful potentate of Kazhdahar, Ahmed-Shah, sent a special task force to defend Tashkent against the Chinese. It was this show of solidarity that forced the Chinese emperor to call off his thrust at Central Asia.

China has by no means renounced these claims to the neighboring territories—a fact that is attested to, in particular, by a good many maps and handbooks published in that country today.

It would, for instance, be wrong to try to find the Caspian Sea on those maps. Instead, one will see the internal lake Lihai, as it was termed in the ancient Chinese maps. The Aral Sea is designated Hsian-Shuihu, Lake Issyk-Kul is Jehai (the Hot Sea), and so forth. As for the Turkic-speaking people of Central Asia, they are part of the Chinese nation which was at one time ruled by the "Heavenly Kahan" of the T'ang dynasty, Tai-Chui (627–649), whose lands used to be called Turkestan. Or so the Chinese historians would have it.

## China Suits Her Actions to Her Words

The efforts of the Chinese Communist leaders to resolve the question of the Soviet territories by military strength go far back in history. As far back as 1930, the CPC leadership made an attempt to adopt a political line aimed at provoking a military conflict between Russia and Japan. Li Li-san, who then stood at the helm of the CPC, believed that the conflict should grow into a world war which, by inflicting incalculable damage upon the Soviet Union, would thus clear the way for the swift progress of the Chinese revolution.

During the Second World War, when the Nazi armies stood at the gates of Moscow, the Russian government hastily appealed to Mao Tse-tung to step up military action against the Japanese forces in order to prevent Japan from striking at the rear of fighting Russia. Mao in effect refused and made not the slightest effort to comply. The prospects of Russia's defeat suited him perfectly. In that event he would have obtained a double victory. On the one hand, with Japan's military effort diverted to the Soviet Far East, China would practically have been left to its own devices. This, naturally enough, would have been a great help to Mao in establishing his domination throughout China. On the other hand, with the elimination of Soviet Communism, the Chinese variety, with Mao at its head, would automatically have become the recognized leader of the world Communist movement.

After the Second World War, continuing the same line, the CPC leaders laid their stakes on provoking a world war between the Soviet Union and the United States. Had they succeeded, China, then a nonnuclear power, could have quietly sat the whole thing out watching its two mortal foes, Russia and America, destroy each other.

Realizing that they were getting nowhere in their bid to bring down Russian Communism by pitting it against Japan, Germany, or the United States, the Chinese Communists finally reached the conclusion that China itself would have to do the job. Awareness of this coincided in time with the start of their policy of preparing actively for war with Russia.

Information about Mao's plans, intentions, and maneuvers must surely have reached Stalin's ears. In all probability, he was quite aware that Mao's victory, while but a local success for the Communist movement, would in the long run carry a threat for the international movement as a whole, and in the first instance, a threat to the citadel of the Communist movement, the Soviet Union. Strategically, Stalin would have preferred postponing a Communist takeover in China to seeing Mao Tse-tung and his group gaining the upper hand in that country. And insofar as it depended on him, that is exactly what he tried to do. As he himself said in a conversation with a Yugoslav delegation, after the war he had insisted that the Chinese Communists join Chiang Kai-shek's coalition government and disband their army. From the standpoint of the Marxist revolutionary, the particularly amazing thing was Stalin's demand that the Communists disband their forces. Stalin's prestige in the Communist world was so great that the CPC representatives, in Moscow at the time, promptly agreed to carry out his instructions to the letter.

Having acceded to Stalin's demand, the Chinese had, however, no intention of complying with it and on returning home, they did exactly the opposite. The outcome and its adverse effect on the Soviet Union and on the international Communist movement are all well known. All the more significant in this context is the foresight which Stalin displayed.

For that matter, another great contemporary of Stalin's, Sir Winston Churchill, showed equal foresight. "The time will come," he said referring to China, "when the world will impatiently bear the existence of great barbaric nations who may at any time arm themselves and menace civilised nations."

Threatening demonstrations on the Sino-Soviet border began very soon after the worsening of relations between the two countries and have never ceased since 1960.

In 1960 over one hundred Chinese herdsmen deliberately violated the border and spent several months on Soviet territory in the area of the Buz-Aigyr mountain pass of the Tianshan Range before being driven out by the winter frost.

In the subsequent exchange of diplomatic correspondence on this subject the Chinese government argued that it did not regard the act in question as a border violation and that the territory concerned was allegedly in dispute. Since then the Chinese government has invariably exonerated all of its nationals, whether civilians or servicemen, who have violated the Sino-Soviet frontier. The culprits themselves have likewise usually refused to leave Soviet territory of their own free will.

The Soviet government statement of September 21, 1963, pointed out that in 1962 alone over 5000 cases of Chinese border violations had been registered and in 1963 over 4000. The decrease was more than made up for by the number of people involved, which had risen to over 100,000.

The clash on Damansky Island did little to cool off the situation. Between June and mid-August of 1969 there were 488 cases of deliberate Chinese violations of the Soviet border and attempts to provoke armed conflicts. Throughout 1970 and practically to this day the situation on the Sino-Soviet boundary has remained in the same state of permanent conflict and unceasing tension. This prelude to full-scale aggression has one other manifestation.

During World War II the Germans tried to determine the area of the most likely invasion by analyzing what parts of the coast British intelligence was most interested in. And they were quite right in their approach. Increased intelligence activity is a sure sign that "something is up." That sign is in evidence today along the entire length of the Sino-Soviet border.

Several years ago the flow of refugees across the border from the CPR to the USSR, which is a customary element of frontier life, suddenly increased. On the face of it, this was attributed to the Cultural Revolution and nothing much was made of it. Understandably, Chinese intelligence decided to make the most of it by infiltrating its agents among the refugees. The aim was only too obvious, since the refugees were allowed to settle in the Maritime Province, Siberia, or Central Asia, that is, the most likely areas of possible conflict.

As soon as the Soviet authorities unmasked some of these agents posing as refugees, they began screening these "Peking enemies" much more carefully. But only in rare instances could even the most sophisticated checking procedures really identify who was who.

With the risk of a Trojan Horse galloping right into their own stable, the Soviets decided it was time to quit the charity game and return all the defectors to China before things got out of hand. It was something that had to be done but only after it was done did it become clear how right it was to have done it. When the refugees were returned to China, some of them began chanting slogans or else shouting violently anti-Soviet slogans. They were the ones who had come with a special purpose and were now proving to their masters they had done their best, but. . . . Others were in despair. Those who had fled of their own free will had nothing to look forward to but the noose. But first they would be dragged through all the frontier villages hung with a placard saying "Traitor" so that others would know the score. Tragic as the fate of these people was, it was the only way the Soviets could curb the infiltration of Chinese agents. Shortly afterwards the flow of refugees dwindled to a mere trickle. And yet there really was a Chinese attempt to infiltrate their agents into Russia, an attempt showing heightened Chinese interest in that particular area of the USSR.

Preparations for a future war also involve the preliminary indoctrination of a country's own population. The Chinese authorities did that—as evidenced, among other things, by the directive of the CPC on Preparation for War in Defense of the Motherland of August 26, 1969. The directive called for the immediate preparation for total war.

After Hua Ko-feng and his supporters came to power, many foreign observers awaited, if not a complete change, then at least an amelioration of the position. But contrary to their forecasts, this did not take place. The summons for war against the Soviet Union are still to be heard from Peking.


## The Aggressor Rebuffed

The Russian explorer P. Chikhachov, who visited the Russo-Chinese border areas in 1843, wrote: "These places can never become an object of diplomatic debate or a theatre of war." The silent forests and deserted mountains must have deluded Chikhachov. Even at the very time he was writing those words, the territory in question had for over one hundred years been an arena of military and diplomatic struggle between Russia and China. We have discussed previously the Far East, Siberia, and Central Asia. China is laying claim to all of them— even though their total area is twice the size of China proper.

In its effort to justify its claims to those territories, Peking is citing such arguments as past cultural or trade links, brief campaigns by Manchu forces, and even the attachment of those lands to the empire of Genghis Khan. The logic of the latter argument is that the Ching emperor Kangshi once declared himself to be the successor of Genghis Khan. Therefore the present rulers of China, who obviously regard themselves as the successors of the Ching emperor, lay claim to the legacy of Genghis Khan.

Peking's expansionist claims toward Siberia, the Far East, and Central Asia go far back in history. The early documents of Russo-Chinese relations bear witness to the start of that expansion. The instructions issued to the Russian envoy to Peking in 1725 included this point: "And also those Chinese declared to the envoy Izmailov that they intended to build a fort on the river Irtysh and to place their troops there. If they should now broach the subject anew, they must be told that the river Irtysh has been within the possessions of the Russian Empire since long ago; on it stand the Siberian town of Tobolsk and many other forts and townships. And therefore Her Imperial Majesty can on no account permit that the aforesaid Chinese build their forts within the possessions of the Russian Empire."

Later, even in the nineteenth century, when the border between the possessions of the Russian and the Chinese empires had already been delimited, the Chinese constantly sent military detachments across the picket line. The Russian authorities sent out Cossack frontier units to meet those detachments and to establish law and order: "After lengthy objections, arguments, and much wrangling, the Chinese would return to their own land." In the case of one such episode it was reported that a Cossack frontier unit had "curbed the audacity and insolent persistence of the Chinese commander and, without firing a shot, had compelled a sizable Chinese detachment to withdraw from our land near Lake Issyk-kul."

Even then the Chinese were seizing any opportunity to precipitate various clashes, seeking to call in question various sections of the frontier line. The Russian authorities did their utmost to avoid conflicts in order not to give any grounds for action of this sort by the Chinese. Thus, K.A. Skachkov, the Russian consul, instructed the military frontier authorities "that our soldiers and guns should not go even one arshyn (less than a yard) beyond the boundary line. And also please warn the officers that the soldiers and Cossacks should behave in an exemplary fashion on the border, without in any way offending the Chinese."

This extremely circumspect policy pursued by the czarist government in the Far East was in marked contrast to what it was doing on its other borders. It would be quite wrong, however, to believe that for this price Russia succeeded in buying the tranquility or security of its frontiers with China for any length of time.

Summing up that policy, one Russian scholar wrote at the beginning of this century: "For several years we have been observing constant friction between China and Russia, with the weakest side, that is, China, always on the offensive, while Russia, undoubtedly far the stronger side, limits itself to a weak defence. Our Policy is built all the time upon compromises, in the ephemeral hope of disarming China by our tractability and complaisance, all of which shows a complete willingness to take into account the psychology of the Asian peoples who are at a certain level of cultural development when, apart from rude force, they recognise no other incentives for correct relationships with foreign states."

This is not an isolated observation. The same conclusions were made by other Russian researchers studying Sino-Russian relations. "We," one of them wrote, "usually went from one concession to another in our desire to see the solution of the question. But at the same time we were unmindful of the fact that the Chinese do not recognise generosity in politics and that in every concession they perceive nothing but the weakness of their adversary. . . . Seeing our constant tractability China came to believe in its nonexistent might and became convinced of our political weakness."

Such observations certainly make one feel that in the Orient a people's national character strongly affects the conduct of external affairs. The national psychology of those responsible for the implementation of foreign policies therefore remains powerful enough to override the leveling effects of doctrines and the bureaucratic apparatus.

And academic circles were not alone in their conclusions regarding the effects of the Chinese national character on China's foreign relations. Shortly before the October Revolution in Russia some leading military and administrative figures also reached the conclusion that a tougher policy should be pursued vis-à-vis China. The governor-general of Turkestan, General A.N. Kropotkin, wrote in 1916: "The future threat to Russia emanating from this empire of four hundred million people is beyond any doubt. As 800 years ago, the most vulnerable portion of the Russian frontier is still that great passage through which the hordes of Genghiz-Khan poured into Europe."

The turbulent developments that ran their course in Russia and China soon after served for some time to blunt the acuteness of the problem of relations between the two countries. For many years China was torn between its civil war and the war with Japan. Under those circumstances it had to lay aside its traditional expansionist policies in the East. No sooner did the situation in China begin to return to normal however than the problem of relations between the two countries rose once again to its full stature. For China it was a problem of continuing its pressure on the East; for Russia it was a question of the measures it could take to offset that pressure.

The switch from endless concessions and tolerance to a tougher line, the necessity of which had been pointed out in Russia even before the October Revolution, was at last made by Khrushchev.

Both China and, indeed, the entire world were shown ample evidence of the firmness of that line during the fighting over Damansky Island and other, less dramatic, armed clashes on the border. The threat of Chinese aggression keeps the Russian troops along the Sino-Soviet border in a state of constant alert. Such tactics are very much in accord with Mao's well-known words: "It is extremely important to keep the enemy in the dark about where and when our forces will attack."

For the Soviets a military showdown is less than desirable. Many Western political and military commentators believe that war between China and Russia is inevitable. Harrison Salisbury thinks so, so do Professor N. Maxwell of London University and a number of other authors. The idea of a war with China has never been popular in Russia. And Russian authors who foresaw the possibility of such a turn of events, invariably emphasized that such a war would have to be forced upon Russia and would in any event be to its disadvantage. "Peace with China," wrote A. Maximov in 1901, "is more desirable for us than war, as we do not need any territorial acquisitions at China's expense. Nonetheless, it is extremely difficult to keep that peace.

"This war," he pointed out elsewhere, "even in the event of complete success, can yield Russia no advantages."

From the standpoint of China's military potential, the perceptible signs of Maoist China's rapprochement with the United States can surely leave no one indifferent. What particularly strikes the eye in this connection is the fact that this rapprochement and Washington's decision to end its ban on sales of strategic commodities came literally in the wake of a drastic deterioration in Soviet–Chinese relations. It takes far less than a professional strategist to see the direct link between the two. The rapprochement and the lifting of the strategic trade embargo came about when the United States saw that China's war machine had its sights trained on Moscow, not Washington. But surely there is something quite familiar about this business of making concessions and strengthening the potential aggressor in order to turn his eventual aggression in the right direction. The historical analogy is all too obvious. A new Munich, this time with China cast in the role of Nazi Germany, would be an attempt to pay off one more claimant to world domination by channeling its aggressive drive toward Russia. Indeed, if Russia has saved Western civilization once before, why not again?

The United States may be able to play "off with the old love, on with the new." Taiwan and China are separated from the North American continent by 6000 miles of Pacific Ocean. But to the Soviet Union, China is the girl next door and neighbors have to be taken seriously.

The U.S. government was quick to deny accusations of wishing to promote an East-East conflict; they maintained that the normalization of United States' relations with China would do much to lift the threat of China, forever abandoned by the West, turning to the Soviet Union for political support. They looked forward to seeing a strong and secure China stabilizing the shaky world. Many consciences were easier to think that close to a quarter of the earth's population were to end their isolation, and rejoiced in reports of an ever-increasing flow of technicians, students, and tourists after the protracted freeze.

It is the very size of China's population that reinforces the Western powers' habitual trend toward a Munichlike policy. Apart from the military-political aspect the predicted growth of China's industrial and military potential has also the implication of the economic incentive it holds out to third parties. For Western economy China with its extremely capacious market could become a lasting cure-all. The possibility of a country like China becoming the essential ingredient for the successful functioning of the capitalist economy was pointed out at the turn of the century by the noted Russian historian Eugene Tarle. In his words China could with time become something like a "safety valve to let off capitalist steam." At no time has that prophecy been so close to the truth as it is today. The $20-billion trade accord which Japan signed with China to run for 13 years is only one of many signs proving its accuracy. There are even instances of the study of capitalist management techniques being advocated.

Certainly, the economic implications of the present situation do not deprive it of its purely military aspect. And as already suggested above, the military aspect hinges on an attempt to turn the rising tide of aggression away from the Western world, notably from the United States, and direct it toward the Soviet Union.

Many people here with whom I happened to discuss this problem (and there are not a few who find it continually nagging at the back of their minds) are sure of the unpredictability of the Chinese, speaking of them as driven by inexplicable motives to make trouble, and therefore allow that an exchange of blows may start at any moment. Such a point of view would permit of some really serious provocative action on the part of the Chinese being interpreted as the onset of aggression. It is difficult to overestimate the scale of the retaliation when those responsible for the decision would have to take the fate of millions of their compatriots into consideration.

So often in the course of world history time has played the part of a healer, but in the case under discussion it is working as an aggravating factor and entirely in China's favor. It is obviously important when it comes to the strength of the army that China may be expected to put into the field. An annual population increase of 15 million means that the potential size of that army is growing at a rate of 30 divisions every year. Even if war should break out today, the Soviet forces would have to deal with an enemy of three or even four times their own numerical strength. True, the Russians are so far considerably superior as regards the quantity and quality of their equipment, but this gap is gradually closing. Some time ago China manufactured no combat aircraft or tanks of its own, but, following monumental efforts, it does today. The modernization plans have included consideration of investment in West European weaponry such as Scorpion and Chieftain tanks, antitank and antiaircraft missiles and Harrier fighters. Some time ago China had no atomic or hydrogen weapons and today it has them. It has the delivery vehicles too, though so far in but limited quantities. Transall transports may solve this problem.

Reports of troop movements from the coastal regions facing Taiwan southwards toward Vietnam but principally northwards toward the long border with the Soviet Union fit in with the opinions of Western military experts. They believe that with the start of hostilities the Chinese Army is expected to strike at the Maritime Province so as to reach Vladivostok, Komsomolsk, and Khabarovsk. But in order to carry out that operation, while at the same time adequately protecting the rest of its territory, the Chinese army would have to concentrate on that key sector no less than 5000 combat aircraft and 50 divisions fully equipped with modern weapons. The International Institute for Strategic Studies finds that 70 of the 136 main divisions of the Chinese army are already deployed in the north.

So if what is for China a disadvantageous gap in military technology and armaments is closing, the other, and extremely favorable, gap in manpower is just as inexorably widening. Therefore, it would be far more difficult to achieve a military victory over China today than it was a decade ago. And it will be immeasurably more difficult in another decade than it is today. One highly placed Soviet official has been reported as saying that it would even be unjust and cowardly to leave the solution of the Chinese question for the next generation to cope with.

Regarding the fighting spirit of the Chinese soldier, there are in fact two opposing viewpoints. Many Soviet military men grudgingly praise his qualities. As one high-ranking officer from the Central Asia military district put it, he "can be stopped by nothing short of a direct hit." A different view is held by some of those who once lived within China's boundaries, mainly Uighurs and Mongols. Most of them have a long personal record of fighting against the Chinese, first the Kuomintang, then the Maoists. In their words the Chinese soldier is a good fighter only for as long as luck is on his side. As soon as the situation changes and the fortunes of war are reversed, he loses his presence of mind.

The contradiction of these two opinions does not rule out the truth of each. It should be remembered that the interior qualities of the Chinese soldier were never more manifest than in the course of punitive or colonial actions or operations against insurgents. It may well be expected, therefore, that in a major war, the outcome of which would determine the destiny of his country, that same soldier would behave quite differently.

On the other hand, an exaggerated assessment of the fighting spirit and capability of the Chinese soldier would be equally unjustified. It is largely based on the experience of border clashes. It is a well-known fact that engaged in these clashes on the Chinese side were special units whose personnel had been specially selected and trained. Like the commandos and the green berets they are not to be mistaken for the army as a whole and should, therefore, be judged accordingly.

The real truth about the fighting qualities of China's regular forces will most likely be found somewhere between these two extremes—probably a little closer to the lower end of the scale.

Past experience has shown that there is a direct link between the fighting spirit of an army and the general mood prevailing in the nation as a whole. Some military experts hold that it is in fact even a reflection and a derivative of that mood. What, then, can be said regarding the sentiments prevailing in the rear of the Chinese armies ranged along the Soviet-Chinese border? By and large, these sentiments are of two different kinds, in keeping with the two main population groups in the area—the indigenous inhabitants and the more recent arrivals from China proper. The fact that the former would eagerly seize just about any pretext to renew or step up their armed resistance is too obvious to be repeated. What the latter, the

Chinese settlers, would do in the event of an armed conflict can safely be predicted by listening to the accounts given by refugees from China; these include Uighurs, Mongols, and even some Han Chinese.

Put together, their story is that as soon as news of the Sino-Soviet border conflict got around, a wave of panic swept over the frontier provinces. Tens of thousands of Chinese settlers hastily took flight, aiming to get as far away from the area as they possibly could. Towns like Altai, Kuldja, and Tarbogotai were virtually deserted. The would-be refugees took already overcrowded trains by storm while others, despairing of finding a foot- or handhold on a train, simply took to the roads and plodded along pushing their carts loaded with their belongings before them. For many hours propagandists in special loudspeaker vans positioned at all the crossroads vainly tried to turn back or at least stem this human torrent. When it became clear that nothing could be achieved through these methods the army was brought in to stop the exodus. For several days in a row hundreds of military trucks forcibly returned the refugees to the places they had just left.

Another event of this kind occurred in the fall of 1970. A refugee from Eastern Turkestan by the name of Gyiny Batyr has been living for many years at Tashkent. One-time leader of a successful anti-Chinese uprising, his name has become legend for many of his compatriots. Today, at seventy, he is old and sick but in popular memory he is still the young and dashing horseman charging at the head of his men into towns from which all Chinese had hastily fled. And the people are still awaiting his return. From time to time the rumor spreads like wildfire through Eastern Turkestan that Gyiny Batyr is leading an Uighur army in Kazakhstan and will soon come to their aid.

Not long ago a Uighur shepherd from Eastern Turkestan tending his sheep near the border saw—or thought he saw—in the mountains several horsemen who soon galloped away. That same day news that one of Gyiny Batyr's advance parties had been sighted spread through the surrounding villages. Unimpeded by censorship, the rumor spread by word of mouth and several days later the whole of Eastern Turkestan was in a state of wild anticipation. The local Chinese settlers sat up and took notice. The first few Chinese to start leaving while the going was good brought down the avalanche. It was the story of what happened during the frontier fighting repeated all over again. And again only the army which sealed all the roads succeeded in bringing the refugees back home.

This overriding urge on the part of the Chinese settlers to leave lands they obviously do not regard as their own at the very slightest sign of danger can surely give the army no great urge to defend them.

## The Mongolian People's Republic: Target of Chinese Aggression

It will be recalled that to the very last the Kuomintang did not recognize the Mongolian People's Republic. Not to mention the fact that it was categorically opposed to the granting of self-determination to these Mongolian people who against their will remained within the administrative boundaries of China.

The Chinese Communists took a no less intractable position on the Mongolian issue. True, here too, as in many other instances, it is a position which has undergone a striking evolution from one end of the scale to the other. The resolution on the national question adopted by the First All-China Congress of Soviets in 1931 emphasized: "The Basic Law (Constitution) of the Chinese Soviet Republic must clearly indicate that all nations within the boundaries of China have the right to national self-determination, including the right to secede from China and form an independent state, and that the Chinese Soviet Republic fully and unconditionally recognizes the independence of the Outer Mongolian People's Republic."

Further confirmation of this stand will be found in the Appeal of the Government of the Chinese Soviet Republic to the Mongolian people issued in December 1935. It recognized the right of the people of Inner Mongolia to form their own government and the right of complete secession.

Then came a change in the Chinese attitude toward Mongolia. The exponent of the new and totally different position was Mao and, insofar as his position begins to be the dominant one of the Chinese Communist leadership, it became the official party line. There was no longer any mention of Mongolia's right to secede from China. On the contrary, the question was how to prevent it. In a conversation with Edgar Snow in July 1936 Mao Tse-tung declared: "When the people's revolution has been victorious in China, the Outer Mongolian Republic will automatically become a part of the Chinese Federation."

In calling the Mongolian People's Republic "Outer Mongolia," Mao was deliberately emphasizing the integrity of the two Mongolias—an integrity, that is, in the context of their inevitable future unification under Chinese authority.

Like the Chinese Nationalists, therefore, the Chinese Communists could never bring themselves to countenance the loss of Outer Mongolia—let alone face any thought of letting Inner Mongolia out of the Chinese fold to join the Mongolian People's Republic. No wonder then, as one American journalist wrote later, "in 1948, when Mao Tse-tung and his Communist followers came to power in China, many people believed Mongolia would again become part of China."

This belief was not only held in the United States. In 1949 Mao Tse-tung very bluntly raised the issue of the return of Outer Mongolia to China in his talks with the Russian leaders. In 1954, some time after the death of Stalin, he took the matter up with the new Kremlin leaders. In both instances, however, Moscow replied that the question of returning or not returning to China—the question of giving up sovereignty or keeping it—was one for the Mongolian people themselves to decide.

In response to attempts to solve the Mongolian problem by the "Chinese" method, the leaders of the Mongolian People's Republic made known their position very forcefully. A statement put out by the Mongolian Telegraph Agency on September 9, 1964, emphasized: "Our people, having achieved outstanding successes in building Socialism, are reaping the fruits of their free and independent existence and they will allow no one to encroach upon their sovereign right. . . . The sinister designs of the Chinese Nationalists to do away with the state independence of the Mongolian People's Republic are absurd and unrealizable."

Equally outspoken was the Mongolian Communist party leader Tsedenbal in his speech at the 1969 Meeting of Communist and Workers' Parties in Moscow. "It is not hard to imagine," he declared, "what a grave predicament the working people of Mongolia would find themselves in if the great-nation designs of Mao Tse-tung were fated to be realized. This can be judged by the oppression and humiliations to which the Mongols, the Kazakhs, the Tibetans, the Uighurs, and the other national minorities are subjected in China and by the rude manner in which their rights and liberties are violated.

"As one of China's neighbors," Tsedenbal went on to say, "the Mongolian People's Republic is directly experiencing the effects of Mao Tse-tung's anti-Socialist policy and it is being subjected to its hostile assaults along a variety of lines. ... Underlying the anti-Mongolian policies and actions of the Mao Tse-tung group are its great-nation chauvinistic claims upon our country inherited from the Chinese militarists and the Chiang Kai-shekists."

---

The unbending attitude of the Soviet Union toward its Far Eastern frontiers undoubtedly has a sobering effect on Peking. Awareness that aggression against the MPR is bound to trigger off a powerful Soviet reaction also serves as a factor restraining China's military activity in the region. In other words, the Chinese leaders have begun to realize that any action they take to unleash hostilities or suppression in the region will inevitably involve China in a total war entailing the use of all means of warfare, including the most destructive ones. The very future of China, and above all, of the leadership that ventured to take that step would then be at stake. By the very fact of its presence the impregnable wall of Soviet divisions deployed in the north ever increasingly deflects the arrow of likely Chinese aggression toward a region which, Peking believes, is far safer—a region south and southwest of China.

# 8

# AGGRESSION TO
# THE SOUTH

Like any body of water which always flows in the direction where it meets the least resistance, the aggressor usually chooses a victim who is likely to put up the least resistance. To the north of China lies the Soviet Union with which a military showdown is fraught with dangerous and far-reaching consequences for Peking itself. But to the south and southwest lie numerous Asian nations whose military potential is immeasurably weaker than China's own. What is more, historically the south and southwest have always been traditional directions of Chinese aggression. The history of the peoples of those countries is a history of unending struggle against Chinese hordes which have constantly sought to subjugate those lands and attach them to the "Heavenly Empire."

Even in its most difficult years, during the civil strife and the war against Japan, China never let these centuries-old inclinations out of its sight. In December 1943 the newspaper *Ishi pao* formulated China's national tasks thus: "In East Asia a vast territory from the Indian Ocean in the west to Japan in the east and from Australia in the south to Alaska in the north will in future entirely belong to China and we shall have to be responsible for the integrity and prosperity of that entire territory."

Also in December 1943 the newspaper *Shishi sing pao (Current Affairs Review)* reported: "After the war China will secure a leading position in the eastern and southwestern Pacific."

The present Chinese Communist leadership has completely taken over that heritage of first imperial and then nationalist China, namely, aggressive designs aimed southward and southwestward. It was in fact none other than Mao Tse-tung himself who adopted and endorsed that heritage. From his work *The Chinese Revolution and the Communist Party of China* it follows quite plainly that Burma, Indochina, Nepal, and Korea are Chinese lands which had been unjustly detached by the imperialists. Naturally, it is China's national task to return those lands. To press home their point the Chinese authorities have published numerous maps which show countries such as Burma, Vietnam, Kampuchea, Laos, Thailand, Nepal, the principalities of Sikkim and Bhutan, some areas of India, and Korea as part of China's national territory detached from it at various times by the imperialist powers.

The aggressive policy pursued by the Chinese Communist leaders toward these territories today is not just a continuation of the line taken by the Ching Empire of old, however. It has some distinctions. Firstly, it is a part of Peking's worldwide expansionist policy; secondly, it is a very long-term policy; and thirdly, it is regarded less primitively than in the past when it is seen as a direct armed invasion. (This last possibility is not, however, totally ruled out by Peking but is treated only as one possible way to achieve the desired goal.)

A subtler, gradual, and covert form of aggression against—and ultimately the annexation of—those territories by China may prove possible, Peking believes, through two factors: the presence in those territories of large numbers of Chinese settlers and the existence there of various pro-Mao groups, parties, and militant insurgent organizations.

The overseas Chinese permanently residing in southeast Asia form a big group indeed: On an average one out of every twenty inhabitants is Chinese. The total number of Chinese settlers in this part of the world is over 20 million.

Wielding considerable economic and, therefore, also political influence in these countries, their Chinese residents are a powerful instrument of Peking's policies in the region. And Peking uses that instrument very flexibly: from financing and setting up antigovernment insurgent groups to conducting Maoist propaganda among the population. As the Peking *Jenmin Jihpao (People's Daily)* reported, "Propaganda of the teaching of Mao Tse-tung is a sacred and inalienable right of Chinese residing abroad."

At this point it would be logical to take a closer look at the methods China is employing today to prepare and carry through its aggression against these neighboring countries.

*INDIA.* The reader will doubtless recall the first Sino–Indian border incident when China began by force of arms to assert its rights to a piece of an uninhabited land in the mountains. A piece of land belonging to China, Peking alleged; a piece of land belonging to India, declared New Delhi. Regardless of the legal aspects of the dispute, however, the Chinese soldiers who shot up an Indian frontier patrol at the same time destroyed the legend of the peace-loving new China. It was then that world—and especially Indian—public opinion saw China for what it really was: an inheritor of the traditional expansionist policy of the Chinese Empire of old, the target of aggression being as always China's closest neighbors.

The rebuff meted out to China on the boundary with India and the tenacious defense put up by the Indian army along its border have prompted China to choose other, more flexible, forms of aggression. A new Chinese drive was mounted to foment separatist tendencies among various tribal and national groups, especially those living close to the Sino-Indian frontier. In the first instance this method was applied to the Himalayan kingdom of Bhutan and the state of Nagaland. There have been many reports in the Indian press about the secret support given by China to the separatist nationalist groupings of the local Naga and Miso tribes. With Peking's support a so-called Revolutionary Government of Nagaland was set up on Indian territory in the area occupied by the state bearing the same name. That "government's" armed gangs made an attempt to unleash guerrilla warfare in the area in full conformity with the classical Maoist concepts and principles. The whole thing actually boiled down to sporadic raids on police stations, offices, and frontier posts. The Peking-inspired war against India on Indian territory failed to meet the support of the bulk of the state's population. Subsequently the self-proclaimed head of the "Revolutionary Government" Skato Swu and 3000 of his followers laid down their arms. Then the Indian press cited many facts culled from the testimony of the luckless insurgents, proving that the disturbances in India's frontier zones were being deliberately and consistently fomented by Peking.

The surrender of this large group of pro-Peking separatists did not, however, restore law and order in this area. Other armed bands guided from abroad are continuing their efforts to detach the area from India. As the *Indian Express* has pointed out, in late 1973 alone insurgent separatist groups of Naga tribesmen received over 50,000 rupees from Chinese emissaries.

Armed groups of Miso tribesmen are equally active in waging an armed struggle under the slogan of secession from India. When captured they usually admit, like the Nagas, that many of them have been given special military training in China following which they were clandestinely sent over the border.

*BANGLADESH.* The Bengali-language and English-language newspapers of Bangladesh have carried numerous reports about terrorist antigovernment actions in that country. Here again it is China that has been rendering military and financial backing to these insurgent groups. The purpose of such activities is to create chaos and instability in Bangladesh and ultimately bring to power a Maoist-inclined leadership. Not content with political provocations, the antigovernment groups have of late taken up arms.

*NEPAL.* Having normalized its relations and expanded its economic ties with Nepal, China is at the same time making every effort to set up and activate various armed antigovernment organizations in that country. In late January 1974 the Nepali weekly *Rashtra pukar (The Voice of the Nation)* wrote that there are entire areas in Nepal where armed Maoists are "terrorizing the population."

*BURMA.* Back in the early 50s a map was published in China depicting a part of northern Burma as Chinese territory. The Burmese government quite naturally sent China a note of protest. And yet in subsequent border talks with the Burmese the Chinese representatives continued to refer to those very maps.

But the Chinese politicians would not have been worthy of their calling had they gone no further than merely indicating their aggressive designs on maps. And, of course, they did go much further. Their next step was to start fomenting separatist and antigovernment sentiments in Burma. This is being done along two lines: through the numerous Chinese community and through the Shans and Karens, national minorities who live in areas adjacent to China.

Many Burmese and foreign commentators accredited in Burma have stated that the Chinese minority makes up the nucleus of all antigovernment disturbances and so-called guerrilla action. "There can be no doubt," the *Far Eastern Economic Review* has pointed out, "that through the Chinese Embassy in Rangoon Peking has deliberately organised provocations and that well trained Chinese cadres in the Chinese community in Burma have instigated trouble." During the suppression of such antigovernment disturbances several hundred Chinese were arrested.

Ideologically the instigation of antigovernment separatist action is carried out either through the extensive flow of Maoist literature sent in from China or through the radio station that styles itself "Voice of the Burmese People." The Burmese authorities have established that the radio station is located in Chinese territory, in the southwestern part of the province of Yunnan. Chinese backing also takes on more tangible and material form: the financing, arming, and training of insurgents. According to some reports which have appeared in the foreign press, there are special military camps in the province of Yunnan where members of antigovernment armed groups are specially trained. From there they use mountain tracks to return to Burma. Their mission is to organize armed raids on local offices and military units, and to carry out sabotage, assassinations, and all kinds of political provocations.

The areas inhabited by the Karens (7 percent of Burma's population) and the Shans (6 percent) are the mainstay of antigovernment separatist action in Burma. After a spate of terroristic acts, raids, train derailments, and the like, Chinese-trained groups of Karens and Shans some time ago mounted regular military action against government forces. At one time they even succeeded in capturing the frontier town of Kuikok. The attackers were supported by artillery firing from Chinese territory.

According to Burmese press reports, armed tribal groups, supported by outside assistance, are trying to set up on Burmese territory something like "liberated areas" along the Burmese–Chinese frontier.

It is an interesting fact that, with regard to Burma, Peking is switching more and more from covert support for the insurgents to overt backing. One confirmation of this will be found in the *Shiche Ditu* (the *World Atlas*) recently published in China by the Ditu chubanshe publishing house. The authors of the atlas quite openly express their admiration for the "immense successes" achieved by the "armed struggle" of the antigovernment forces in Burma.

*MALAYSIA.* As in all the other countries that Peking has chosen as targets of its covert or overt aggression, Maoist political and extremist groups have been set up in Malaysia. One of their more "innocent" forms of activity is the propaganda of the "Chinese road to Socialism" and of Maoism.

The same objective of creating tension and fomenting antigovernment sentiments is served by the provocative broadcasts of the "Voice of the Malayan Revolution," a radio station located in China. Additional proof of Chinese support for this antigovernment campaign was provided by the establishment in Peking of a permanent mission of the so-called Malayan liberation league. The evidence seems to point to Peking's desire to instigate an armed struggle to overthrow the legitimate government in Malaysia as it has elsewhere in the region. Malaysian newspapers have cited many facts that this is indeed so, one of the latest being a report about a Maoist military training camp discovered by security forces in the state of Perak.

*THAILAND.* Thailand has no common frontier with China. While this certainly makes it more difficult for Peking to instigate subversion in that country, there is, nonetheless, an insurgent movement there too, whose members, according to the London *Weekly Review,* undergo training in China.

As in other similar situations, proscribed subversive organizations in Thailand have enjoyed not only the support of but also the official recognition of Peking. Permanent missions of the Thailand liberation movement and the Thailand patriotic front have been set up in China. And in this case, too, an antigovernment broadcasting station, which, on behalf of the "people of Thailand," calls for the overthrow of the legitimate government, is situated in the Chinese province of Yunnan.

*SRI LANKA.* In contrast to other countries where insurgent and separatist movements operate under Peking's auspices, there were no signs of any such movement in Sri Lanka for several years. There did exist various pro-Peking groups such as the so-called People's Liberation Front and various Maoist publications and Chinese literature were disseminated. And that seemed to be all. No one knew, however, that deep in the jungle hundreds of men were being trained in guerrilla tactics and in handling modern weapons—in order to be ready to use those weapons at the appointed hour.

That hour struck in April 1971. Thousands of men armed with tommy guns suddenly emerged from the jungles in various parts of the country. It was later calculated that there were ten attacks for each policeman. Not surprisingly, dozens of police stations were routed. According to figures provided by the Sri Lanka military command, the strength of this underground army was something like 10,000 men with another 30,000 support personnel. The government with its tiny army of 6700 men proved powerless. Within several hours the administration and the entire system of law and order were paralyzed.

Under these circumstances the Bandaranaike decided to take the one and only step open to it: It turned to the governments of other countries for help. And such help was forthcoming. Soviet transport planes brought in armaments and ammunition. Soviet MIG–15 fighters appeared together with two large helicopters to serve as troop carriers. Five manned helicopters arrived from India and another two from Pakistan. Six more were hastily bought in the United States and eighteen in Britain. Transport planes carrying armaments arrived from Belgrade and Cairo. In addition, India sent 153 Gurkhas who were charged with guarding airfields. Indian naval vessels began intensively patrolling the island's coastal waters to cut the antigovernment forces off from their source of supply.

Faced with this resolute counterattack, the movement fell apart at the seams, died down, and went back underground. The Sri Lanka press later emphasized that the value of this experience gained at such great cost was in the conclusion that antigovernment military conspiracies stemming from Peking can be thwarted if they are opposed by the solidarity of Asian and other nonaligned nations.

THE PHILIPPINES. Like Thailand, the Philippines have no common boundary with China. And also as in the case of Thailand, this has not helped them avoid dangerous "attention" on the part of Peking. For many years a variety of Maoist political groups have been active in the country and as everywhere else they were given Chinese support and aid, including financial assistance. In recent years the more extremist of these groups, following the line taken by others of their ilk elsewhere, have been going over from political activity to armed subversion. In March 1969 the establishment of a "New People's Army" as an armed wing of the "Mao Ideas Communist Party of the Philippines" was announced. This "army" proclaimed the start of an "armed revolution" whose aim was to seize power. According to the Philippines' press the "army" is mainly made up of Chinese and is financed by Peking. The activities of these armed groups and their program differs but little from the operations of similar groups directed by Peking elsewhere in Asia.

*VIETNAM.* In 1789 the Chinese made an attempt to conquer Vietnam; it ended in the rout of the Chinese. But memories of that invasion are so deeply imbedded in the minds of the people that the victory is still annually commemorated by the Vietnamese. It is also very much in the minds of the Peking leaders but they take a rather different view of it. The fact that Chinese forces once overran Vietnamese territory is seen there as meaning that this area historically belongs to the "Celestial Empire."

The present Chinese leaders have never renounced Chinese claims to Vietnamese territory. On the contrary, they have reiterated them on more than one occasion. A direct reference to this will be found in Mao Tse-tung's *The Chinese Revolution and the Communist Party of China.* In January 1974 these historical claims suddenly assumed concrete and real form: Chinese naval vessels after some bitter fighting captured the Paracel Islands belonging to South Vietnam. Despite the wave of indignation that swept over neighboring Asian nations the Chinese flag is still flying over this portion of Vietnamese territory.

In this connection, the *Times of India* has expressed just apprehensions that, given these ambitions, "the entire basin of the South China Sea will de facto find itself under Chinese jurisdiction and all other nations will be refused the right to carry out explorations for oil, gas, and other resources in the area."

Citing his conversations with diplomats from several Southeast Asian nations, the correspondent of another Indian newspaper, *The Indian Express,* wrote that they were all "frightened by Chinese military actions."

The Indonesian newspaper *Pedoman (Guardian)* has indicated that Peking's action is seen in Indonesia as plain evidence of the Chinese leadership's desire to resolve all disputed issues through the use of force. "The armed clash around the Paracel Islands," reports another Indonesian newspaper, *Sinar Harapan (The Ray of Hope)*, "graphically shows the Asian nations what methods Peking will resort to in the future in this part of the world." The newspaper *Brita buana (News of the World)* has pointed out that China has several territorial claims upon its neighbors. And it asks whether Peking may not be out to follow the precedent of the military action it has taken for the solution of other problems of this kind in the future.

These assessments are probably typical of what must be uppermost in the minds of Asian public opinion generally. Characteristic in this respect is the reaction of the *Japan Times*. China, according to that newspaper, has shown its aggressive claws and it has plainly indicated its readiness to use armed force to establish control over lands it is claiming as its own. The seizure of the Paracel Islands is obviously a continuation of the belligerent line that was manifest during China's border clashes with the Soviet Union and India. Southeast Asian reaction to the visit of Chinese Vice Premier Teng Hsiao-ping to Thailand, Malaysia, Singapore, and Burma at the end of 1978 was keenly watched by East and West and whether the Chinese considered his achievement to be a limited success or not, there is no doubt about the fact that he was received there with understandable caution.

━━━━━━

The conclusion to be made from all this is that China wants to revise virtually all of its boundaries with virtually all of its neighbors. What is more, China is laying claim not only to the territories directly adjacent to it but also to those situated much further away. To achieve these goals—inherited by the present Communist leaders of China from imperial China—a two-pronged method is employed. While maintaining normal diplomatic and other contacts with the governments of neighboring nations, Peking is at the same time supporting, arming, and inspiring antigovernment and separatist movements in their territories. The aim of these movements is either to detach a portion of these territories which could subsequently be placed under Peking's control or to carry out the forcible overthrow of the legitimate governments and replace them with pro-Peking political groups.

The incompatibility of such practices with commonly recognized international standards should surprise no one. In a way it is traditional. As one Russian scholar pointed out at the end of the last century, "China does not recognise European methods in diplomacy, it does not recognise the sanctity of compacts and treaties, as it has already proved many times over, most frequently to Russia."

World public opinion is becoming increasingly aware of the geographical direction of present-day China's aggressive inclinations. "Hardly anyone can doubt the aggressive aims of China's policy, notably in respect of its southern frontiers," emphasized the Beirut newspaper *Ash Shaab (The People)* on January 30, 1974.

There would seem to be only one thing that could counter that aggression: the unity of those nations that are its target—a unity which could assume some form of collective security in the face of the imminent threat.

# ♤ PART III ♠

It is a fact that Soviet-Chinese relations leave their imprint on the demographical and economic processes in Siberia and the Far East. On the other hand, the future of the outlying national regions of China—like the future of China as a whole—is not indifferent, to say the least, to what goes on over their borders. By this token, what is going on in those areas today increasingly predetermines what the Soviet and Chinese representatives will say to each other tomorrow. The future of relations between the two powers, the Soviet Union and China, is today being decided not only in Moscow and Peking but also in places like Vladivostok, Khabarovsk, Blagoveshchensk, Frunze, Tashkent, and Alma-Ata. This dependence becomes all the more imperative if what is happening is regarded not as the end result but as a fragment in the historical process. And surely this is the only method that can be accepted by a commentator claiming to be objective and convincing.

Thus, these remote territories, which have traditionally acted only as the object of international law and of the policies of the big powers, are now themselves beginning to play the part of the subject of events.

This is definitely the conviction I have formed after my long pilgrimage along the Sino-Soviet frontier—from the Ussuri River to the foothills of the Pamirs.

# 9

# NORTH OF THE AMUR

## Over the Demographical Barrier

There was a time when the vast continent lying to the east of the Urals was for Russia an immense demographical vacuum. One exiled revolutionary, who saw much of the area at firsthand, wrote in a letter home: "The environs of the Western Siberian road which I have just travelled (1,300 versts, from Chelyabinsk to Krivoshchokovo, three days) are amazingly monotonous: a bare and desolate steppe. Neither dwellings nor towns. . . ." Neither dwellings nor towns. This observation is often repeated in the letters and diaries of other exiles, travelers, and officials who had been in those parts. One did not have to be a Lenin (and the words quoted above are indeed his) to notice how sparsely populated the area was in comparison with European Russia. But one certainly had to be a man of Lenin's mentality to think of the consequences of this fact—consequences which may take effect in twenty, fifty, or even one hundred years. This is why the former exile-turned-head-of-government promptly directed his attention to the task of settling the Far East and Siberia. The revolution and the civil war were hardly over when at Lenin's command thousands of over-crowded trains began chugging their way to the East. On the return trip they were empty. In those years 4 million peasants settled in the new lands.

But that was only the beginning. Throughout the following decades a concerted effort was made to keep the stream of migrants flowing steadily toward the Pacific coast.

It was a policy that bore fruit—though perhaps a bit less than could have been expected. In the relative (not the absolute) sense the results are quite impressive. Since the 1917 revolution Russia's entire population has increased by half as much again. But Siberia has registered a twofold growth and the Far East a fivefold one. This resettlement policy had several distinctive features about it. For one thing, the immigrants found themselves in almost totally uninhabited territory so there was no problem of friction with the indigenous population. For another, those native tribes that did live there were dependent on no neighboring state.

The Russian explorer V.D. Poyarkov wrote of the peoples living in the middle and lower reaches of the Amur: "The Natkas live along the Amur on both sides in Uluses, and pay no one any tribute." This sparseness of population and independence of the local tribes were also emphasized by the Russian ambassador in China, I.G. Spafary: "Here and there roam the free Mungals and Tungases, and they pay tribute to nobody."

Therefore, in virtue of these specific conditions, the Russian settlers did not destroy anyone's statehood or way of life or take away the local people's land. In marked contrast, the arrival of settlers on the other side of the border brought with it the destruction of the state entities of the Manchu, the Mongols, the Uighurs, and the Tibetans, while the indigenous population was forced into the mountains or onto unfertile land and their national culture was either destroyed or assimilated.

Furthermore, it was not a migration of people belonging to just one nationality. A sizable proportion of the immigrants were in fact non-Russians: mainly Ukrainians.

Another interesting feature was the geography of the new settlements. Before the revolution the new arrivals made their homes mainly along the Siberian and Far Eastern borders. These were the so-called Trans-Baikal and Amur cossacks.

For St. Petersburg these settlements were like the gold-prospector's stakes with which he marks off the area he lays claim to. Furthermore, by settling along the border and tilling the land, the cossacks, through the very fact of their presence, acted as a kind of demographical barrier against the expansion of the Ching Empire.

After the revolution the character of the resettlement changed completely. The settlement of frontier areas ceased to be the prime objective of the authorities. The stream of immigrants was now regulated not by considerations of building up a demographical barrier on the boundary with China but by economic considerations. The very concept of "settling the territory" is now seen as implying not the building of settlements along the border (by now this had become a thing of the past) but the fastest possible economic development of the territory.

In place of the purely quantitative criterion (depending upon the number of immigrants) came a much more sophisticated one, the qualitative criterion, depending upon the nature of the settlement.

The immigrants now streamed not southwards into the areas situated along the frontier but northwards into areas with far more severe climatic conditions and totally lacking in communications yet vastly more promising in terms of economic development. Within a fairly limited space of time ore-dressing plants, mines, metallurgical plants, and factories were built. In keeping with the new objectives, the population in the northern areas started increasing seven times as fast as that in the areas bordering on China.

A certain role in the intensive development of these areas was, of course, played by Stalin's concentration camps. For decades hundreds of thousands of prisoners, armed with only the most primitive technology and working under the most horrifying of conditions, built roads, erected industrial plants, and laid the foundations for the future economic prosperity of the territory virtually on the bones of their comrades. The death of Stalin and the ensuing events brought all this to an end. The prison camps were emptied and the Siberian wind and weather uprooted the barbed-wire fences and the watchtowers. The abandoned construction sites were left to the mercy of the snow and the rain. Naturally, only a few of those who had been brought in under guard evinced any desire to stay of their own free will. Those who did were mainly ex-prison guards and administrators who feared the consequences of a chance encounter with their former wards. It was as if some hidden mechanism of vengeance were at work: Free to go anywhere, they preferred to stay on forever, dooming themselves to voluntary exile in a place where they had but recently been so zealously guarding the captivity of others. But even if these people amounted to hundreds, they could not provide a solution to the manpower problem.

If the official population statistics of the eastern areas had included the prison-camp inmates, the years following the death of Stalin would have been marked by a sharp depopulation of the Far East.

It proved quite a problem to induce a voluntary large-scale influx of migrants into areas which had for so long been associated with hair-raising stories of punishment and forced labor. But there was more to it than the psychological barrier. Even the Chinese threat has only recently dawned on the popular Russian consciousness.

According to available statistics, the real income per capita in the Far East was between 15 and 17 percent higher than in Moscow and the central areas of European Russia. And even 40 to 42 percent higher than in the Volga valley area. At the same time the cost of living in the Far East is about 35 percent higher. Until recently, the one offset the other; so there was no point in moving from one place to the other just for financial gain.

Having exhausted all their methods of propaganda, persuasion, and publicity, the authorities finally resorted to what they should have done in the first place—the introduction of material incentives. In January 1968 a system of material benefits was brought into effect which included among other things a bonus of 20 percent on the basic wage. In some areas the bonus runs as high as 50 percent—or even 150 and 200 percent.

The system seemed to work. For a time it looked as if in another decade or two the size of the population in these areas bordering on China would increase two- or threefold. But even today it seems certain that this will never happen. The very system of material incentives that had produced an influx of people into the outlying areas became the cause of a no-less-intensive outflow. Though sometimes reaching a very high figure indeed, monetary earnings did not always bring the earner the consumer goods and services available in the more developed parts of the country. Hence the tendency, once a large sum of money had been saved, to move back to European

Russia. Commenting on this tendency, one Soviet sociologist has observed wryly that the bank account acts as a balloon which raises a man and carries him away to more comfortable surroundings.

True enough, within the first three years, having saved quite substantial sums, half of the immigrants emigrate. The migration has, in fact, become two-way, with the number of people streaming out of Siberia exceeding the influx of new arrivals. The situation of so-called negative migration has arisen and in some places there is even a resultant shortage of manpower.

The general outflow of the population is compensated for only by the birthrate. It follows that in recent years there has been no sharp population increase in the territories adjacent to China. Nor is there any reason to anticipate any drastic change in the situation over the coming years. Characteristic in this respect is the very moderate population projection for western Siberia: 1959, 11.2 million; 1970, 12.8 million; 1980, 15.5 million. For eastern Siberia the figures are: 1959, 6.4 million; 1970, 7.4 million; 1980, 8.3 million. And for the Far East they are: 1959, 4.8 million; 1970, 5.8 million; 1980, 9.0 million. In other words, the projected population growth in the Far East and the whole of Siberia between 1970 and 1980 is set at only approximately 8 million people.

One of the indicators of the extent to which a territory is populated is the density of population. Comparing the population densities on both sides of the border, we obtain the following picture: China—6 people per square kilometer (Eastern Turkestan), 10 people per square kilometer (Inner Mongolia), 50 people per square kilometer (Tung pei, formerly Manchuria); average: 33 people per square kilometer. The USSR—an average of 4.7 people per square kilometer (the Amur and Khabarovsk regions, the Maritime Provinces, Kazakhstan).

Thus, there is today a fairly powerful demographical pressure emanating from China. It is a result of a forceful resettlement policy that has been pursued ever since the time of the Ching emperors.

The fact that the Soviets are not countering this pressure with at least comparable demographical pressure on their side of the border is by no means a sign of lost opportunities; it simply indicates a fundamentally different approach to the problem. It is a dead certainty that if the Soviets really thought a drive of this kind to be essential, Moscow could find the ways and means to move tens of millions of families to its eastern frontiers. If this is not being done, it means Russia feels it undesirable to build up demographical countertension in the frontier areas. The Soviets are opposing the feudal concept of "developing a territory," that is, by way of its "dense settlement," with a concept prompted by modern conditions and the scientific and technological revolution. In the Soviet book a "developed territory" is an "actively employed territory." And it is from this viewpoint that the Soviets are today regarding the future of the territories bordering on China.

## The Economic Aspect

It is bizarre to recall that in 1923, during Lenin's lifetime, when the first All-Russian Agricultural Exhibition was opened in Moscow, Siberia was represented by nothing more sophisticated than butter, furs, and sawed timber. Yet it is a fact. It is just as much a fact that today Siberia produces the most intricate of machine tools, turbines, presses, and generators, all of which are sold to sixty countries and that in the future there will be an even more striking output increase.

This brings up again, and far more acutely, the problem of manpower—that is, the people who will have to do it all. On the face of it, an increase in production should require a proportionate increase in manpower. This is by no means so, however. With the advent of the scientific and technological revolution the rigid dependence of the volume of production on the size of the work force, which used to be an indisputable law, loses its validity. Commenting on the contemplated industrial upsurge in Siberia and the Far East, Academician Marchuk formulates this concept thus: "More and more manpower resources can of course be recruited. But this is hardly the only or the most reasonable method. It is a fact that a considerable portion of Siberia is not very cosy, and it is not a very easy place to live in. What is more, its main wealth is situated in places that are not easily accessible. It is therefore necessary, in our view, to develop the economy in the area on the basis of practically fully automated new enterprises, on the basis of the extensive use of electronic computers for management. . . ."

As one of the leading figures in the Siberian branch of the Soviet Academy of Sciences, Marchuk is not just speaking for himself. This is the fundamental economic concept of the administrators of the eastern regions.

"If the money that is spent today on recruiting manpower was given to us in the form of new technology, the need for such recruitment would long since have been obviated," one such administrator told me. His words were echoed by many others whom I chanced to meet.

"We are spending enormous sums of money to organize the transportation of a worker from the European areas to Siberia or the Far East," another told me. "We pay the fare for him and his family, we pay all his traveling expenses, we provide him with accommodations, food, and cultural facilities. He works for us for a year, two years, maybe three. And he gets a bonus wage all the time. Then he leaves and with him goes all the money we've spent on him. Now, if we had instead spent the money on the development and production of mechanisms capable of replacing that worker, our investments would not leave the territory and we could long since have been getting by on our own."

The idea of replacing men with machines and mechanisms is by no means new. The significant thing here is the publicity it has been given in the press—and specifically in the context of one part of the country, the eastern areas. Quite apart from the question of economic expediency, this surely looks like a declaration of the demographical policy to be pursued in regard to the territories bordering on China.

Sound economic arguments are adduced in favor of that policy. Academician N. Nekrasov has written that in climatically unfavorable areas the substitution of mechanisms for one single worker in a basic industry actually means the release of ten people when one counts members of his family.

It is hard to imagine that the mechanization and automation contemplated in these areas could ever produce a surplus of manpower or even an outflow of the population. But it is surely obvious that they will reduce to a minimum the need to import manpower from outside the territory. Actually the process has already started. The shortage of manpower in the eastern areas is already resulting in a faster introduction of new technology in comparison with the rest of the country. In the last decade industrial production in the Far East has grown 200 percent while the population has increased by only 20 percent. So the increasing development of Siberia and the Far East is ceasing to be merely a question of resettlement policy. It is becoming more and more a question of technology and power supply.

As regards power resources, the eastern areas are practically inexhaustible, exceeding by far anything available in the well-developed European areas of the country. But today these areas, which contain nine-tenths of the nation's power resources, account for only one-fifth of its industrial output. The task is to eliminate this economic disproportion.

With this in view, it is planned to secure a faster rate of economic development in the eastern areas than in the rest of the country. In their calculations the planners are proceeding on the assumption that the population influx into the area will be negligible. The expected increase of industrial output is therefore based exclusively on the steady growth of power production. A good deal has been done already. Two examples are the Bratsk hydropower station with a capacity of 4 million kilowatts and the Krasnoyarsk plant with a capacity of 6 million kilowatts. The amount of electric power per capita in Siberia today is three times as high as in the rest of the country. This gap is bound to go on widening with the construction of several new power stations, each with a capacity of between 4 and 6 million kilowatts.

It is also planned to build in the lower reaches of the Lena River a giant power station with a capacity of between 15 and 20 million kilowatts. The aggregate capacity of all these power plants will amount to some 50 to 60 million kilowatts.

On the basis of this cheap electricity (it costs only half as much as electricity in European Russia) are planned several powerful industrial complexes in the eastern areas: oil and chemical plants in the vicinity of Tobolsk and Tomsk, an aluminium plant in the Sayan Mountains, and completion of the construction of the Krasnoyarsk aluminium plant and the Zimin electrochemical plant.

The anticipated rate of economic development in the territory is characterized by these figures: The planned rate of industrial development in the Far East in 1971–1980 is 150 percent higher than in the European part of the country and the construction of twenty or so new electric power plants in the area will treble the output of electricity. In the same time period eastern Siberia will increase the output of electricity fourfold, the output of steel twelvefold, and the production of chemical fibers eightfold.

The abundance of primary products, cheap electric power, and advanced technology (necessitated by the shortage of manpower) all help to cut production costs.

The sharp increase in industrial output (without any marked population influx) is expected to entail a substantial improvement in living standards. It has in fact been calculated that by 1980 per capita consumption in western Siberia will be doubled. This faster rise in living standards in the eastern areas may in future encourage more people to go there. But this is not the only, and now no longer the major, consequence of the accelerated economic development of the territory. From what I have seen and heard in the Far East and Siberia, I venture to suggest another likely implication.

## The Possible Consequences

Economists and economic executives in the eastern areas are becoming increasingly convinced that it is historically unfair and economically unjustified to regard the Far East and Siberia merely as an industrial and raw materials appendage to European Russia. They feel that the territory is sufficiently insular and self-reliant to develop by itself, in accordance with its own specifics. This desire for economic self-reliance and independence on the part of the central authorities, situated as they are thousands of kilometers away, was reflected in the idea of the export specialization of the Far East which was advanced by a group of scientists. Their arguments centered on two main points.

On the one hand, the development of the eastern areas is largely held back by the resources and requirements of the European part of the country. This is why the deposits of titanium–magnesium sands in Kamchatka, Sakhalin, and the Kurile Islands are not being developed. The gas, marble, and iron ores of Sakhalin are lying idle, waiting for the time when they can hold their own in competition with other and more conveniently located deposits. This is also the reason why the richest copper fields in the world, at Udokan, have been so slow in their development. Moreover, even those industrial goods and raw materials that are produced there have to be exported to the European area because the local market just cannot consume them. But the high cost of transportation frequently renders such shipments economically unjustified.

On the other hand, the Far East lies next to areas which could become unlimited markets for its products. "The Far East is situated close to the lively sea routes linking Asia with the American continent and numerous ocean islands," one economist from Khabarovsk has emphasized. "About one-half of the world's population lives in the region." The proposed reorientation of the territory's economy from west to east presumes the accelerated development of export-orientated industries and the invitation for that purpose of foreign capital.

The orientation of the eastern areas on external ties would obviously solve the food problem in the territory. For one thing, the production of food locally is fairly expensive: Potatoes and other vegetables cost twice as much and milk and meat half again as much as in European Russia. For another thing, the territory does not meet its food requirements anyway. According to some late figures, the Far East meets only 32 percent of the people's demand for meat, 30 percent for milk, and 19 percent for eggs. Deliveries of food from abroad would solve the problem and remove the need to ship eggs, meat, and vegetables all the way from the Ukraine, the Baltic region, or the northern Caucasus.

At first this concept of the economic development of the eastern areas met with no opposition from Moscow. This is evidenced by the decree of the Central Committee of the Communist party and the Soviet government passed in 1967: "On Measures for the Further Development of the Production Forces of the Far East Economic Region and the Chita Region." The decree specifies in particular the task of developing those branches of the economy which allow an increase in the volume of foreign trade with the countries of the Pacific.

In keeping with this line, a Soviet–Japanese Economic Cooperation Committee was set up, with the Japanese extending 154 million dollars' worth of credits, Japanese timber-cutting equipment appeared in the forests of the Far East. The immediate result was a rise in labor efficiency and the volume of exports. In just ten years labor efficiency in Far Eastern forestry was doubled—largely due to export ties with Japan and to Japanese equipment.

According to Far Eastern economic executives, for reasons of limited local demand and the expediency of shipment to the European areas of Russian there has been no need to increase the production of timber. Yet the production is growing fast—commensurately with rising exports. In western Siberia, however, with its limited export outlets, there is a constant glut of timber. Even logged timber is piled up in vast quantities waiting to be shipped out. In the coming years the export capacities of the eastern areas can be increased to the maximum.

The export mindedness of the eastern territory's forestry authorities is naturally contingent on return imports of goods which are in short supply. With this in view, the Japanese trading organizations and the Far East have established relations of so-called "coastal trade." The Khabarovsk Trading Society was specially created in Japan to handle this trade. On the Soviet side these matters are dealt with by Dal'intorg, also a specially established agency.

A no-less-powerful link which has bound the economy of the Far East closely to the overseas demand is the export of fish. On the Soviet side the export requires almost no additional investments for any processing of the catch for the Japanese are more than willing to accept the fish right on the high seas, from ship to ship. Several fishing boat captains in Vladivostok have told me that even today so much of the catch goes to Japan that in effect "trade with Japan is the mainstay of the entire Far Eastern fishing fleet." If this remark is considered against the background of the limited refrigeration and canning facilities of the Far East, it will sound all the more plausible.

And so, two major branches of the economy—forestries and fishing—are already flourishing, thanks to their orientation primarily upon the external, not upon the domestic, market. It is now the turn of the others: mining, engineering, and heavy industries.

At an economic conference in Khabarovsk in the spring of 1964 the need was emphasized to build in the Far East an integrated metallurgical plant. This, the conference affirmed, was a paramount condition for the development of engineering orientated on export to the countries of the Pacific. All told, it is planned to increase Far Eastern exports 3.5 times—and this relates to exports not only of timber and fish but also of machinery, oil products, iron ore, gas, coal, and ferrous metals. With this in view, work is already under way to develop the port facilities at Vladivostok, Vanino, and Nakhodka. The construction of a new seaport is also in the blueprint stage.

The advocates of the export orientation of the Far East see these ties as being especially important since they have not only an economic but also a foreign policy effect: They promote the stabilization of international relations in the area.

It is an interesting fact that the local population of the Far East and eastern Siberia is far from indifferent to growth of external economic ties. For them this not only means Japanese transistors and knitwear in the local shops. It is also a symbol of their territory's status in international affairs. They know perfectly well that foreign-made goods can appear only in exchange for locally manufactured products. So when they see foreign-made goods, they also see a confirmation of the importance and the high quality of their own output. This form of indirect praise feeds local patriotism, which is always open to the slightest excuse for self-affirmation.

It is a curious fact that when anyone in the Far East starts talking about the foreign-made goods on sale in the area, the mention of Japan is immediately followed by a reference to China. Not, however, to list the goods that country is selling but to voice regret that in recent years "the Chinese have completely stopped trading with us." This is certainly true for in the last decade Russia's volume of trade with China has dropped seventeenfold. Yet every time some Chinese-made goods do appear in Blagoveshchensk or Khabarovsk, public opinion is swift to react. A long time after—as much as a year or two—they will tell you exactly when the local department store sold Chinese towels or thermos flasks.

The contemplated export orientation of the economy may be regarded as a kind of flexible concession system where the investment is made not at the initial stage and not in the extraction or processing of the product, but rather in its final price (which naturally includes the cost of the extraction, the processing, and the transportation). It is only too natural that from the purely geographical standpoint the starring roles in this system should belong to both Japan and China.

But while China, in the grip of monetary political considerations, is letting the golden opportunity slip through its fingers, the Japanese traders are not only making the most of it but will also do their best to collect what would otherwise—in a different political situation—have by rights gone to China. Unlike political situations, which are liable to change within days or even hours, the structure of established economic ties is a far more stable mechanism. So the economic relationships that are taking shape between the Far East and the neighboring territories today are here to stay—with all the advantages for those who are involved in them and all the disadvantages for those who are not.

It is true, however, that lately certain signs seem to have appeared indicating that Moscow is not too keen on the idea of the economic development of the Far East as a separate entity. Should this be taken to mean a departure from the tendencies that seemed to have been predominant? The answer to that question requires a look into the past.

Throughout Russia's history Siberia and the Far East have always been a home for individuals antagonistic to the central authority. They were either exiles, that is, people who had repudiated the dominant social system, or resettlers, that is, people who had been rejected by that same social reality and compelled to seek refuge as far away from it as possible. This traditional antagonism toward central authority was invariably present here in every manifestation of mass consciousness: jokes, folk songs, tales, and even rumors. Under the Soviet regime, when enormous towns arose in Siberia and the Far East, with all the attributes of civilization, the inherited feeling of antagonism was reinforced by an involuntary inferiority complex. This was something that had never existed previously for the conditions of life in the territory could bear no comparison with the "civilized" areas.

Another destructive component of the mass consciousness is the memory of attempts by Siberia and the Far East to secede from the "central authority." Far back in czarist times a whole host of Russian governors in Siberia had conducted themselves most independently, even going so far as to issue their own money, decide on questions of war and peace with neighboring states, and completely disregard the orders emanating from the throne. The situation sometimes reached the point of armed clashes between the troops of the recalcitrant local governors and the forces specially sent in from St. Petersburg.

This desire for independence and secession was carried into effect as soon as Russia was rent asunder by the revolution and the civil war. It was then that the Far Eastern Republic came into being. Unlike the establishment of Soviet power in European Russia, where such events as the seizure of power, the execution of the czar and his family, etc., were sanctioned only after the fact by legal acts, all that occurred here was from the very outset in complete accord with law and order. "By the will of the entire people," read the Act of the Government of the Far East, "expressed at the Conference in the city of Chita through the representatives of the united regions of the Far East, in pursuance of the Declaration of 29th October of this year, the entire territory from the Baikal to the Pacific Ocean is hereby declared the independent Far Eastern Republic."

Hastening, as it were, to emphasize its independence from the rest of Russia, the new government promptly introduced its own monetary unit, created its own army, and adopted the Constitution of the Far Eastern Republic (approved by the Constituent Assembly of the Far East on April 27, 1921).

But the days of the Far Eastern Republic were numbered. When the Red Army (which had come to her aid to repel the Japanese intervention and the army of Kolchak) reached the Pacific coast, Lenin uttered his famous words about the Far East being "our land all right." These words became the epitaph of the Far Eastern Republic. Its founding fathers and leaders were gradually reduced to mere executors of decisions handed down from Moscow and in the end they simply vanished from the political arena one after another.

The orientation of the eastern areas on the adjacent foreign lands and even on Latin America breathed some new life into the ghost of the former independence. And though the economists and executives of the eastern areas are quick to affirm that there is definitely no question of the territory's economic independence, Moscow does not seem to be very much inclined to believe them.

This carefully concealed mistrust thrives not only on the memory of past attempts to achieve independence. Even today the discerning eye can observe some highly meaningful nuances. One feels, for instance, that in areas directly bordering on China, the local authorities frequently tend to soft-pedal the situation so as to avoid possible complications and friction. There are signs that they sometimes take the initiative in various actions or more often restrictions whose aim is "not to irritate the Chinese."

Thus, at Blagoveshchensk, where the Amur is fairly narrow and the Chinese side is in plain view, tourists are recommended to refrain from using their cameras because the Chinese might resent the lenses focused on their territory.

The islands on the Amur belong to the Soviet Union. Most of them are uninhabited and the meadows are used by the collective farms only for hay. The Chinese frequently try to steal a march on their neighbors. On such occasions the hayricks become the scene of stormy arguments under the watchful but inactive gaze of frontier guards on both sides of the river.

"Though right is on our side," the chairman of one collective farm told me, "we usually yield to them. Our people understand that you don't go stealing other people's property unless you're pretty hard up. And they're peasants just like us. And neighbours too. . . ."

You will not hear such words in Moscow. I decided not to ask him outright and compel him to lie to me but I am fairly sure he does not report to the authorities all the incidents involving the Chinese. His main concern and that of the territory's administrators is to preserve at least a vestige of the one-time good relations. They are neighbors, after all. . . .

It was obviously the same considerations that guided the leaders of Kazakhstan when they forbade a group of Uighur refugees to burn publicly a portrait and an effigy of Mao. It is clear that such a demonstration would have changed nothing in relations between the two countries. But from the standpoint of relations between Kazakhstan and China, in Alma-Ata they then decided it would be undesirable.

So even today there are signs of some specific, albeit weakly expressed, relationships between those territories and China. There are some differences with Moscow, albeit minor ones, in regard to China—differences between the general line laid down in Moscow and the toned-down interpretation of that line in the areas concerned. Clearly, in future, with the strengthening of the economic self-reliance of those areas, the nuances may assume a more distinctly etched outline.

It must be emphasized, however, that this confrontation of economic concepts does not affect the sphere of politics or ideology. The dispute is focused on the methods of achieving the most effective economic development of this part of the country. Moscow's position in the dispute is quite clear. It is in favor of a steady and planned advance, an advance based on "consciously maintained proportions," as Lenin put it. Moscow disapproves of the attempts by one territory or another to thrust too far ahead, since if it became the thing to do, this practice would inevitably result in disproportion and economic chaos. This view can be appreciated only too readily. But so can the opposing theory.

Some economic executives in Siberia and the Far East feel, however, that discussions on this topic are somewhat senseless. The steps already taken in orientating the economy of the territory on export ties are irreversible. This applies not only to the all-important fishing and timber industries. There is a widespread belief that even the obvious surplus of electricity being produced by Siberia's power stations today is by no means a miscalculation of the planners but a far-reaching design. And there have already been some voices raised in favor of exporting cheap electricity from Siberia to power-hungry Japan.

Just as one cannot reverse the development of all the branches of the economy, it is quite impossible to abolish such a centrifugal center as the Far Eastern Center of the USSR Academy of Sciences at Vladivostok. Combining under its roof many territorial research institutes, it constitutes a transitional link on the way to the establishment of a Far Eastern Branch of the USSR Academy of Sciences, such as exists in Siberia. Set up under the chairmanship of A. Kapitsa, a Corresponding Member of the Academy, the Far Eastern Center is guiding the work of such research bodies as the Institute of Chemistry, the Institute of Automation and Management Processes, and the Pacific Oceanological Institute.

The movement has gone too far to be turned back. Nonetheless, the situation is rather a controversial one. On the one hand, Moscow is vigorously advocating the development of export-orientated industries. On the other, Moscow is not too favorably disposed toward such moves in the Far East. But this attitude, even if it should not change (and there are indications that it is beginning to do so), can only slow down the process—slow it down so as to coordinate it with the plans, trends, and rates of the economic development of the country as a whole.

The territory's next-door neighbor—the minority-inhabited areas of China—will with every passing year become more and more aware of the economic advantages they have missed. But for some time the doors will still be open. The utilization of those opportunities by the neighboring territories will depend on when the forces opposing Peking in the national areas can begin to carry out an independent policy—a policy in the interests of and leading to the goals of their own peoples.

Undoubtedly, the prospect opening up on the other side of the border for the national minorities' territories in China can only serve as one more factor accelerating the events that are bound to occur there.

# 10

# AT CHINA'S WESTERN FRONTIERS

The desolate mountains walling off the western frontiers of China form a natural watershed between two of the most ancient of the world's civilizations—the Central Asian and the Han. At times the dynamic balance in which the two have subsisted through the ages has been tipped. With bloodcurdling yells hordes of slant-eyed horsemen would suddenly stream down the western slopes of the mountains to overrun the neighboring oases and valleys. But the great distances, the waterless camel trails, and the implacable hatred of the natives would soon dampen their ardor. The sons of the "Celestial Empire" would go back over the mountains, leaving the neglected graves of their less-fortunate warriors to be silted over by the sands until they were level with the surrounding plain. And then all would be quiet again—and motionless—as if nothing had happened to upset the scales of history.

Only once did the two civilizations really break the monotony of the regular and barely detectable oscillations of their contours. This was when part of the Central Asian cultural–ethnical region, Eastern Turkestan, found itself on the inside of the neighboring region—China. In the context of great historical destinies, however, this episode was not really very much more than the exception that proves the rule. The forces straining to restore the balance are far too powerful for the resultant anomaly to freeze into a state of permanence. The reconstitution of the ethnical community is certainly being encouraged by the processes under way on the other side of the border in Central Asia.

The processes at work in the Soviet Central Asian republics go right across the border and to say that they are less than striking—particularly against the dismal background of underdevelopment in the neighboring independent countries—would be an understatement.

Demographically, Central Asia is the zone of highest population growth in Russia. In the last sixty years the population density in the area has trebled or even quadrupled. In terms of economic development, the annual production increment in Central Asia is between 20 and 25 percent higher than in the rest of the country.

Considering the subject matter of this book, however, I want to single out for special emphasis one other process which is very much in evidence in this area directly bordering on China—the tendency toward its general and comprehensive integration into a single and closely knit community.

This means that in the coming years the situation on the western frontiers of China will undergo a striking change. No longer will China's neighbor be just Kazakhstan or just Tajikistan individually— neither of which can ever hope to stand up to a comparison with China by any standards. In their place will be a powerful industry and a tolerably high standard of living, occupying a territory big enough to match China's. This is bound to mean that in this part of the world Central Asia will become much more of a political counterweight to China that it ever was in the past.

## Toward Cultural Unity

As you walk out of the railway station at Tashkent, the capital of Uzbekistan, you will see in the square facing it a monument dedicated to the memory of the fourteen Turkestan commissars who were shot by the czarist counterinsurgents in 1919 at the time of the civil war. But why Turkestan, the traveler may well ask himself. And his puzzlement would be only too natural for since the 1920s the word "Turkestan" has simply disappeared from the official Soviet lexicon.

This taboo was imposed because the word itself is more than just a geographical name. That one word embodies the concept of uniting the entire Moslem-inhabited Central Asia. With the establishment of the Soviet regime and the setting up of national republics, the slogan of such Central Asian unity was branded as counterrevolutionary and anti-Soviet.

In the past the ethnic communities on whose basis these republics were formed had had neither a clearly defined national consciousness nor any previous experience of autonomous statehood. The khanates and bekdoms that once dotted the entire region came into being quite regardless of any tribal or ethnic boundaries. They would arise, flourish and fall, only to arise anew, always within boundaries that were fixed by successful conquests, advantageous treaties, or victorious coups.

Finding themselves within the administrative confines of separate republics, the ethnic communities began swiftly to acquire the features that may be interpreted as "national distinctions." This process of the evolvement of national distinctions is easy to understand considering the rapid efflorescence of culture, literature, and the arts which began in the area at the time. Developing on a local basis, within the enclosed confines of each individual republic, this process could not fail to bring out in the first instance the features of dissimilarity. This self-identification through dissimilarity has traditionally been the way for a new nation to assert itself in relation to its ethnic surroundings.

Yet no characteristic intricacies of the "purely national ornament" or distinctions in dancing steps could ever mask or obliterate the underlying singleness of the cultural and historical traditions. Though the territory of Central Asia is today divided into several ethnic communities, its history and its culture have remained immune to division.

Throughout its history the Central Asian civilization has evolved as a single and indivisible complex. There has never been any separate history of the Kazakhs or the Uzbeks or the Kirghiz. There was one common historical trunk going down to a common root, the ancient Turkic epoch. Today's administrative divisions and boundaries have no justification whatsoever in terms of the region's history. And another thing shared in common—and quite indivisible—are the cultural relics of the past, such as the ancient Turkic runic scripts.

The fact is that prior to the fifteenth century the Turkic people were never once divided. Naturally enough, this singleness of history and culture sometimes gives rise to some curious and amusing incidents today.

One of the ways in which a nation that has only just come into the external attributes of statehood seeks to assert itself is by looking back over its "great and glorious past." Central Asia has been no exception. At one time the authorities in Tashkent, Frunze, Alma-Ata, and Dushanbe launched a campaign to name streets and erect monuments in honor of great men and heroes of the past. At the height of the campaign, when someone took it into his head to see how things were going, he was surprised to encounter everywhere identical monuments and street signs repeating the same names over and over again. This discovery caused a shock and confusion in all the Central Asian capitals. During the ensuing row everyone started accusing everyone else of having unlawfully seized title to his very own great forefathers. Moscow had to intervene and act the role of referee—but it was a difficult job and a thankless role.

Indeed, to what nation should belong, for instance, a poet who was born on territory that is today a part of Tajikistan, but who lived in a locality that is today a part of Uzbekistan, yet who wrote in a language that is closest of all to the modern Kazakh? It stands to reason that the Kazakhs, the Uzbeks, and the Tajiks each think of such a poet as their very own classic and national pride which they have no intention of sharing with any neighbor. To offend no one, Moscow resorts to the judgment of Solomon and pronounces him lawfully belonging to all.

This common cultural heritage of the peoples of Central Asia sometimes extends even to the modern Turkic-language writers. Thus, the noted poet Abai Kunanbayev is regarded as a classic writer of both Kazakh and Kirghiz literature. He is read in the original in both republics. Similarly, the Kazakh writer Abai is read untranslated by the Uzbeks. So it is really hard to say whose writer he is, the Kazakhs or the Uzbeks. And, vice versa, the Uzbek, Navoi, is more frequently read in Turkmenistan and even in Azerbaijan than in Uzbekistan. And the poems of Fizuli, a native of Azerbaijan, are read and sung, untranslated, in Uzbekistan more frequently than in the land of his birth.

In short, notwithstanding the administrative boundaries dividing Central Asia into several republics, the region is in fact a single cultural conglomerate extending from the western frontiers of China to the Caspian Sea. In recent years its unity has been tending to become even stronger. Ties between these republics in the realm of culture and the arts have long since exceeded the level of contacts usually designated as "cultural exchanges." Externally this intensive interpenetration proceeds through two channels: reciprocal guest performances and television.

Every year the cultural administrators of the Central Asian republics get together informally in one of their capitals to draw up a general plan of exchanges of opera and dancing groups, soloists, films, and so on. Only those districts and towns that are left uncovered by this plan are given over to guest performers from Moscow, the Ukraine, or the other republics. In this way priority is always given to cultural contacts between the Turkic-speaking Central Asian republics.

The same principle goes into the preparation of publishing plans, television programing, and theater repertoires. Characteristic in this respect is the repertoire of the Khamza Theater in Tashkent. Out of six plays, only three are by national Uzbek authors. Out of the remaining three one is by a playwright from another Central Asian republic, one is by a Russian classical writer, and the third is a West European classic. Under a tacit agreement among the republics, the same arrangements are made by all the Central Asian theaters, which invariably include in their repertoires plays by authors from the neighboring republics.

As for television, its role in this cultural togetherness is particularly important. The closeness of the Turkic languages makes understanding no problem and since the capitals are not very far apart, the viewer can easily select any program that suits him. And as there is no prophet in his own land, the Uzbeks often prefer to watch programs emanating from Ashkhabad, the Kazakhs from Tashkent, and the

Kirghiz from Alma-Ata. And so the circle of cultural interpenetration closes.

There is, of course, no real way to measure the intensiveness of this process. But on the basis of their own practical experience some cultural administrators in the region believe that in the last five years the intensiveness of this cultural exchange has doubled.

"As time goes on, mutual contacts in Central Asia may be expected to increase still further," one of them told me. "We are quite obviously moving toward a kind of single culture, a single art. As you know, the Leninist nationalities policy proceeds from the prospects of the drawing together and eventual merger of nations. It is surely logical to expect that this process will run its course all the faster among nations that already have a lot in common in terms of language and history. Don't you agree?"

I certainly do.

## The Root of It All

According to the traditional formula of Marxist political economy, all of the foregoing constitutes the "superstructure" or the derivative of the "basis," that is, a derivative of the production relations and of the economy. How then do matters stand in regard to the basis itself which lies at the root of everything? It will be seen that here the forces pulling the region together into a single integral whole are even more powerful than appears on the surface.

This urge is dictated by expediency. It is dictated by the need for the integrated solution of Central Asia's industrial and economic problems. The problem of electricity, for instance, cannot be resolved as a separate Uzbek or a separate Kirghiz problem. Uzbekistan cannot deal with the problem of water resources separately from Turkmenistan or Tajikistan. These common problems provide the incentives for the construction of such common projects as the Toktogul irrigation scheme covering 2 million hectares of land in Kirghizia, Uzbekistan, and Tajikistan or the gas pipeline which supplies three capitals—Tashkent, Frunze, and Alma-Ata—with gas from Bukhara.

The belief that Central Asia should be treated as a single industrial and political complex occasionally gains the upper hand even at the center of power, in Moscow, and then the appropriate organizations and bodies are set up, such as the *Sredazburo* (Central Asian Bureau) of the Central Committee of the Soviet Communist party, which was only abolished with the ouster of Khrushchev, or the Central Asia economic region, or the Central Asia Department of Gosplan (the State Planning Commission), which met the same fate. A reflection of the same tendency was the publication in 1964 in Tashkent of the first and only *National Economy of Central Asia in 1963* annual or the magazine *National Economy of Central Asia*, which also ceased to exist.

Also dating back to 1964 is the publication in *Pravda* of an article signed by the presidents of the four Central Asian Academies of Sciences. The article emphasized that the industry meets the requirements of the region "regardless of its administrative division."

"Regardless of its administrative division. . . ." One does not have to be an expert on Central Asian affairs to grasp the implications behind that formula. Indeed, the article, written, as it were, on behalf of the four Academies, came to be a kind of manifesto of Central Asian unity. According to the authors of the article, the need has now arisen to pool all scientific research throughout the Central Asian region. Named among common problems were the building up of a single power system and the elaboration of a scheme for the development of the chemical industry and for engineering.

This pooling of the scientific and intellectual resources of the republics was, the authors felt, supposed to mark the further drawing together of the Central Asian nations and lead to their unity. Though, after their brief airing in *Pravda*, these ideas were later pointedly forgotten, the memory of them lives on in Central Asia—just as the idea of the future unity of the territory is still very much alive.

And though after 1964-1965 the joint Central Asian economic, planning, and scientific centers were abolished, the idea of unity proved far more difficult to abolish.

A good deal of research is still being carried out on problems affecting the region as a whole: *The Development of the Economic and Cultural Cooperation of the Republics of Central Asia* by Tuichiyev, *Important Tasks of the Scientists of Central Asia* by Yu.V. Zakhidov, *The Development of Hydrogeology and Engineering Geology in Central Asia, What Our*

*Scholars Are Working On* (our scholars being the philosophers of Central Asia), etc.

Scientific conferences are also held quite frequently, such as the Ashkhabad conference on problems of the development of philology in Central Asia or the conference on the development of the water and fisheries resources of Central Asia.

But most important are the annual unofficial meetings of the presidents of the four Academies at which they coordinate the joint work of their colleagues. One such meeting at the end of 1970 adopted a program for the joint long-term projection of the utilization of the natural and manpower resources of Central Asia by the year 2000. Another similar joint projection scheme already underway relates to the less distant future, 1980.

Central Asia is not the only region in the Soviet Union with a penchant for strengthening internal ties. Others include the Baltic region and Transcaucasia. But nowhere else do the economic, scientific, and cultural ties constitute such an integral whole. Neither the Baltic region nor Transcaucasia are so ethnically uniform as Central Asia.

There exists the Council for the Study of the Natural Resources of Central Asia. A similar council exists for Transcaucasia. In the Transcaucasian council the chairman is rotated annually to give each republic—Armenia, Georgia, and Azerbaijan—a chance to be represented in turn. This practice is not followed in the council of Central Asia. There the chairman's nationality makes hardly any difference. This little detail, insignificant as it may seem, is in fact very meaningful. It indicates that integration has already come very close to overcoming one of the principal barriers in its way—the national barrier.

———

Central Asia's progress toward integration will undoubtedly be a powerful external impetus for strengthening the centrifugal forces that are straining to tear China apart. This applies particularly to Eastern Turkestan. In a united Central Asia it will find an additional magnetic pole pulling it out of the vise of an alien and inimical ethnic community.

# EPILOGUE:
# THE LIKELY
# PROSPECTS

All of the preceding boils down to two basic points.

1. The present Chinese leadership, continuing the traditional imperial expansionist line, is laying claim to vast areas of the Soviet Far East, Siberia, and Central Asia.

2. For several decades the peoples of the outlying regions of China all along the Sino-Soviet border have been waging an unrelenting struggle for their national self-determination and independence.

Somewhere along the line these two points meet. The granting of independence to the peoples of Manchuria, Mongolia, Eastern Turkestan, and Tibet, apart from bringing about a just solution of the nationalities question, would largely remove the threat of Chinese expansion toward the adjacent territories. This outcome as a solution of the issue has its history. Having come up against the problem of Chinese expansion, the Russian government from the very outset sought to fence itself off from China with a barrier of buffer states. The first attempts of this kind go back to the year 1722. The Russian ambassador wrote to his government from Peking with reference to Djungaria that "this neighbor could with time become Russia's defense against the Chinese and a most useful ally and therefore it would be all to the good to have a good relationship with him." To that end "artillery captain Umnikovsky" was dispatched to Djungaria. His instructions were to make overtures to the ruler of Djungaria should the latter express a desire to make contact and to promise him protection against Chinese encroachments, protection both diplomatic and military.

Russia regarded its relations with Manchuria in the same light. As one Russian scholar put it, the conversion of Manchuria into a kind of barrier "would yield the immediate advantage that we would fence ourselves off from a hostile China. . . . The history of Russia's diplomatic failures in China in recent years should convince us that the territorial isolation from China should be regarded as Russia's main task. Only in this way can we rid ourselves of a neighbor who is so far merely unpleasant but who can in future become very dangerous."

The same purposes were served by several plans to create a belt of Russian settlements in Manchuria. As A. Kokhanovsky wrote, the purpose of this demographical barrier would be to prevent the Chinese wave from "engulfing our lands."

It is highly noteworthy that even after the advent of Soviet rule the same concept of setting up a system of buffer states around China was advanced by Lenin. Receiving a delegation of leaders of the People's Revolutionary Party of Mongolia, Lenin especially emphasized Mongolia's role, as he put it, as a kind of buffer.

Lenin's idea has by no means lost its significance even today. What is more, in the present-day international situation this concept could relate not only to Mongolia but also to an entire chain of independent state entities which could arise out of China's outlying territories. A token of the realization of those peoples' desire for independence is provided by the centuries-old tradition of statehood which all those peoples have as well as their unending struggle against sinification and for their national self-determination and independence.

Future developments will show how soon the national aspirations of the Manchu, Mongols, Uighurs, Tibetans, and other non-Chinese peoples who today are incorporated territorially in China can become reality.

# INDEX